Published by Jossey-Bass
A Wiley Imprint
989 Market Street, San Francisco, CA 94103-1741   www.josseybass.com

Jossey-Bass books and products are available through most bookstores. To contact Jossey-Bass directly call our Customer Care Department within the U.S. at 800-956-7739, outside the U.S. at 317-572-3986, or fax 317-572-4002.

Jossey-Bass also publishes its books in a variety of electronic formats. Some content that appears in print may not be available in electronic books.

**Library of Congress Cataloging-in-Publication Data**

Dotlich, David L. (David Landreth), 1950-
   Head, heart, and guts: how the world's best companies develop complete leaders / David L. Dotlich, Peter C. Cairo, Stephen H. Rhinesmith,
      p. cm.
Includes bibliographical references and index.
   ISBN-13: 978-0-7879-6479-5 (cloth)
   ISBN-10: 0-7879-6479-4 (cloth)
   1. Executive coaching. 2. Leadership. 3. Executive ability. 4. Excellence. 5. Employee selection.
I. Cairo, Peter C., 1948-  II. Rhinesmith, Stephen H.  III. Title.
   HD30.4.D673 2006
   658.4'092—dc22                                      2006005274

Printed in the United States of America
FIRST EDITION
HB Printing    10 9 8 7 6 5 4

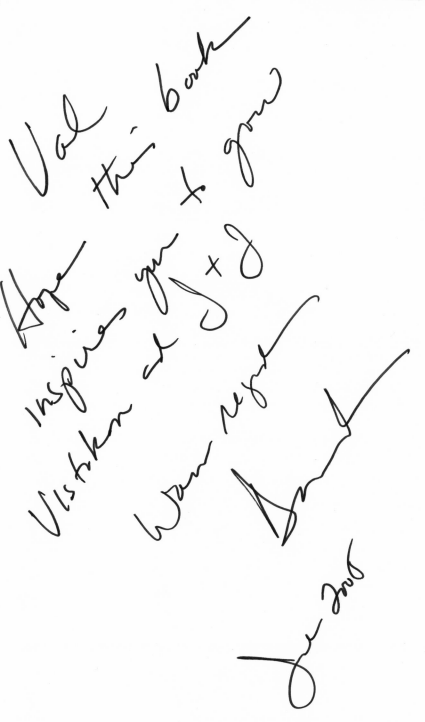

# Head, Heart, and Guts

## How the World's Best Companies Develop Complete Leaders

David L. Dotlich

Peter C. Cairo

Stephen H. Rhinesmith

JOSSEY-BASS
A Wiley Imprint
www.josseybass.com

# Contents

## Part Four: Guts Leadership

## Part Five: Mature Leadership

# Head, Heart, and Guts

# Introduction

Complex times require complete leaders. Partial leaders struggle during an era of paradox, ambiguity, and unpredictability. To employ a one-dimensional leadership approach may have worked in simpler times, but in an environment of moral complexity and rapid shifts in attitude, social and political circumstances, economic conditions, and technology, leaders must be capable of using their head, their heart, and their guts as situations demand.

## What's Wrong with Partial Leadership

In recent years, political, religious, military, and business leaders have all disappointed their constituencies. President George W. Bush exhibited guts in his aggressive strategy to fight terrorists, but his critics have accused him of lacking judgment and compassion in his policy on the war with Iraq. Catholic church leaders may have dealt with the problem of priests abusing children with compassion for the priests, but most people are disappointed by their apparent lack of concern for the victims and their unwillingness to take a strong stand on punishment and restitution. Business leaders have been extremely savvy in delivering short-term results, but they have not demonstrated the inner fortitude and courage to consistently do the right thing in the face of competing stakeholder needs, the constant pressure for performance, and the requirement to keep people engaged and motivated at work.

In other words, our leaders often rely exclusively on a single quality—head *or* heart *or* guts. Unfortunately, when you do that you ignore other aspects of what is required to be successful. If all you are trying to do is demonstrate your analytical rigor, you may come across as insensitive and unethical. Perhaps even more significantly, you will lack the ability to respond effectively outside a narrow range of situations. When you're trying to create a compassionate culture, you may miss opportunities that a more astute and strategic leader would have seen. Relying solely on the courage of your convictions and toughness may cause you to underestimate the negative consequences for the people you are trying to lead.

*New York Times* columnist David Brooks astutely pointed out the failures of institutional leadership in an opinion piece shortly after Hurricane Katrina struck New Orleans. Though his initial focus was on the lack of compassion and execution on the part of the Bush administration toward residents of that flooded city, he noted that this leadership failure was part of a larger trend. Referring to baseball's steroid crisis, corporate scandals, and the military's mistreatment of prisoners at Abu Ghraib prison, Brooks noted how the public has lost confidence in leaders in the same way they did during the seventies.

As executive development consultants and coaches, we have observed this same trend in organizational life, and the cause is partial leadership. We have listened to CEOs as they bemoan the lack of whole leaders in their ranks and express their fear that people no longer trust them. They ask: "Is it possible to develop cognitive abilities, emotional intelligence, and courage in leaders who are deficient in one or two of these areas?"

We have been asking the same question, and the result is this book. Over the years, we have committed ourselves to helping senior leaders develop their head and sometimes their heart. More recently, we have been focusing our attention on the additional requirement for courage—guts—though this remains an area where we (and everyone else) need to do much more work. Still, everything we do in our work and see in the larger world tells us that it is possible to develop whole leaders, but only if organizations move away from traditional cognitive development models and embrace a more holistic approach.

## Who We Are

We're getting ahead of ourselves. We'd like to go back a bit and tell you more about who we are and how we created the three-part model—the head, heart, and guts model of leadership—that you'll find in these pages.

First a mea culpa: as consultants, we have contributed to the problem of partial leadership. We have done our share of classroom teaching, and no doubt our efforts have helped emphasize cognitive skill as the critical component of leadership success. Fortunately, we have also learned from our mistakes, and we discovered that even the most brilliantly analytical leaders fail if they lack certain other, noncognitive qualities. In fact, in our (David and Peter's) earlier book *Why CEOs Fail,* we found that some of the brightest top executives we studied lacked awareness of their personal vulnerabilities, and this lack of awareness resulted in their downfall. In other words, chief executives who possess the emotional capacity to understand themselves and their effect on others, along with cognitive skills, have a much better chance of being successful leaders.

We began emphasizing the importance of "softer" qualities to compliment the "harder" ones. We found that leaders who allowed their vulnerabilities to show or who extended trust before it was earned—what we termed "unnatural" leadership skills—frequently were more effective in certain situations than the traditional command-and-control leaders. We created a development approach that helped leaders develop both cognitively and emotionally.

But something was missing. Each of us glimpsed what it was in our own way and through our own experience. Steve, who has extensive global management experience and was special ambassador to the Soviet Union for President Reagan, observed that in leaders such as Mikhail Gorbachev and Ronald Reagan, what made them effective was their ability to put their beliefs on the line. Peter, as the former head of the Counseling Psychology Department at Columbia University, has consistently worked to develop in leaders the capacity to empathize and connect; he was a first-hand witness to Mayor Giuliani's courage after 9/11 and to how it helped a city cope with despair and fear. David, as a former executive vice president of several large companies, including Honeywell International, worked directly with some of the smartest CEOs but saw that the key to their long-term success, as well as respect and commitment from others, was their willingness to do what was right rather than take the easy or politically expedient course of action.

## What We Stand for and Teach

Guts is an umbrella term for the quality we'd been missing: a willingness to do the right thing, no matter how difficult that is. It became clear to us that leaders who combine the capacity to exhibit courage with cognitive and emotional intelligence are best able to deal with the complexities that organizations face today. It isn't guts in the sense of reckless risk taking that is important; rather, it is the willingness to take risks, based on strong beliefs and values.

This insight is not new or unique, but it is needed now more than ever. Once we began to expand our own understanding of effective leadership, we began testing it out with different companies and leaders, and we have found the response to be overwhelmingly positive. Executives in all types of companies facing all types of different situations quickly saw that the head, heart, and guts ideal, however described, was worth trying to select for, coach toward, and develop.

We are fortunate to work every day with some of the best leaders in some of the top companies in the world, and our clients and colleagues in these companies have contributed to our thinking and insights. We work with them as faculty in senior executive programs that we conduct through the Mercer Delta Executive Learning Center and serve as their coaches and business advisers. They come from a range of companies, industries, products, and services, and they form the basis for our head, heart, and guts approach. Clients include Johnson & Johnson, Avon Products, Bank of America, Novartis, Time Warner, Colgate Palmolive, Coca-Cola, Washington Mutual, UBS, Nike, Dell, Cemex, Mitsubishi, Unilever, and Citigroup. We'll refer to a number of these companies and their leaders in the chapters that follow.

We should also note that our epiphany about the importance of head, heart, and guts leadership paralleled the growth of our own consulting business. Early in our careers as leadership development experts, we felt the need to emphasize the linkage of leadership performance with the hard skills of strategy, finance, marketing, and production, which were typically taught in business skills. When we launched our own executive development company in the late 1990s, we recognized that what distinguished us from the business schools was our ability to integrate emotional intelligence with cognitive skills through assessment and coaching. Soon our business took off, and we grew beyond our wildest expectations to become the leading provider of customized in-house executive programs.

We recognized, however, that leadership development must be linked to organization change in order to sustain learning, and in 2004 we sold our business to Mercer Delta and formed the Mercer Delta Executive Learning Center. In this capacity, we have had the chance to work on significant change requirements for clients, linking leadership learning with the larger issue of organizational change and creating alignment and insight up and down the leadership pipeline. We believe the requirement to find new ways to connect leadership learning with sustained cultural and organizational change is the future of executive development and the way leadership education will stay relevant. To lead change requires guts, and this is where our understanding of the need for guts crystallized.

## A New Way to Approach an Old Subject

We need a fresh perspective on leadership and a fresh approach to leadership development. Without it, organizations will continue to replicate the leadership that exists, churning out more leaders who rely heavily on their cognitive skills but who are ill-equipped to deal with issues that are becoming increasingly complex and confusing daily. When we see a CEO or political leader who demonstrates vulnerability or compassion or who steps up to take full accountability for an error in judgment or execution, we are often so surprised that we hail the person as a great leader.

More so than ever before, CEOs and other executives are managing complex situations and constituencies that will require them to demonstrate a broader range of leadership attributes. They are encountering decision points for which there are no "right" solutions. They will be confronting paradoxes and learning to manage them rather than trying to resolve them. They will need to learn to act counterintuitively at times and to trust their instincts in other instances.

Dealing with these difficult and ever-changing situations isn't possible without head, heart, and guts. Moreover, a "head" leader can't become a whole leader by taking a course in ethics or receiving some coaching on integrity. A "heart" leader isn't going to start taking the right risks by going through a rocks-and-ropes course. Development must be ongoing and multifaceted.

By that we mean leadership is a combination of experience, training, and coaching. In the following pages, we suggest the best ways for organizations to capitalize on experience, training, and coaching to produce whole leaders. Specifically, we discuss leadership traits we have identified through teaching and coaching thousands of leaders around the world. We believe that these are the important traits for future leaders to develop in order to integrate head, heart, and guts.

## Contents of This Book

We have arranged the contents of the book as follows: "Part One: The Case for Whole Leadership" (Chapters One and Two) provides background and context for the methods we describe in the rest of the book. Following that are "Part Two: Head Leadership" (Chapters Three through Six), "Part Three: Heart Leadership" (Chapters Seven through Ten), "Part Four: Guts Leadership" (Chapters Eleven through Thirteen), and "Part Five: Mature Leadership" (Chapter Fourteen), which makes a strong case for the value of developing mature leaders "prematurely," along with instruction in methods for doing so.

Our approach to leadership can be outlined as follows:

*Head Leadership*

- Rethinking the way things are done
- Reframing boundaries when necessary
- Understanding the complexities of a global world
- Thinking strategically without losing sight of short-term goals
- Looking for ideas inside and outside a company, wherever they can be found
- Developing a point of view

*Heart Leadership*

- Balancing people and business needs
- Creating trust
- Developing true compassion in a diverse workplace
- Creating environments in which people can be truly committed
- Knowing what's important
- Understanding and overcoming potential derailers

*Guts Leadership*

- Taking risks with incomplete data
- Balancing risk and reward
- Acting with unyielding integrity in spite of the difficulty
- Tenaciously pursuing what's required for success
- Persevering in the face of adversity
- Not being afraid to make tough decisions

Clearly, many of these traits aren't the traditional focus of leadership development. Even the head qualities are different from the usual cognitive skills such as decision making, strategic planning, and the like. We're not suggesting that traditional skills are unimportant. In fact, we're assuming that any leader who follows a traditional path through business school and into entry-level positions with any company will acquire these cognitive competencies eventually. Our point is that they are no longer sufficient.

We recognize that not all traits are trainable or coachable. For instance, if you lack the innate capacity for integrity, no approach, no matter how effective, is going to help you develop it. We also realize that some traits can only emerge after people go through a series of experiences, fail at some of them, and learn from those failures.

We are assuming that, given sufficient time, most leaders will gain experience and learn from it. We are also sufficiently optimistic to assume that companies will become increasingly perceptive about hiring and selecting people with whole leadership potential. Although they make mistakes or are occasionally blinded by an impressive MBA or other graduate schooling, companies are recognizing the value of hiring future leaders who can empathize and who possess strong values, demonstrated in multiple and unique ways, as well as those who are graduate school stars.

Using examples from our work, case histories, occasional references to research in the field, and suggestions for putting this development process into practice, we make a case for whole leadership. Earlier we referred to a book we wrote called *Why CEOs Fail*. In a very real way, this book is our "antidote" to that one. This book could be called *Why CEOs (and Other Leaders) Succeed*. We trust that it will open your mind to a new leadership model, move you to grasp some of the crucial people issues that are emerging, and inspire you with stories of those who have taken risks based on beliefs and values.

Ultimately, we hope that the book will not only improve organizational leadership effectiveness but expand every individual reader's own leadership capabilities. We also hope this book will help you share our excitement about the possibilities of head, heart, and guts leadership.

## The Scarecrow, the Tin Man, and the Cowardly Lion

We know that the importance of these three human qualities—head, heart, and guts—has been recognized by people before our own time. The idea is not new. The most obvious illustration of it comes from the movies. Almost everyone has seen *The Wizard of Oz*, one of the most popular films ever made. You will recall that the three main characters (besides Dorothy and her dog Toto) were the Scarecrow, the Tin Man, and the Cowardly Lion. The Scarecrow was searching for brains, the Tin Man for a heart, and the Lion for courage—or head, heart, and guts. Each recognized that he was incomplete. Each was searching for the missing piece that would make him whole. Each had an underdeveloped capacity but either didn't know it or didn't know how to use what he had.

We find that many business leaders today are in the same situation as the Scarecrow, the Tin Man, and the Lion—searching for the key personal quality that will somehow make them successful or whole (and often investing significantly in "wizards" who promise to do so). Quite often, what they need already exists within them but is unrecognized or undeveloped. We hope this book will help move you down the yellow brick road of leadership understanding.

◆ ◆ ◆

We don't believe that this book is the last word on head, heart, and guts leadership. In fact, it's the first, and our goal is help you think about this subject in a new and provocative way. We begin, in Chapter One, by building our case for the value of whole leadership in today's fast-moving business world.

# Part One

# THE CASE FOR
# WHOLE LEADERSHIP

# 1

# WHOLE LEADERSHIP VERSUS PARTIAL LEADERSHIP

To be a leader in today's business environment, you need to use your head, demonstrate heart, and act with guts. This is not an unrealistic objective, in that most people are fully capable of exhibiting all three qualities in given situations. Unfortunately, the majority of executives have either come to rely on one capacity or they live in organizational systems that do not reward or reinforce them to develop others. They remain partial leaders, even when their organizations require whole ones.

Why this is so is a combination of history and training. Historically, business leaders have led with their heads—the notion being that if you analyze a situation, absorb the data, and decide among rational alternatives, you can be a strong leader. Generations of MBAs have been trained using these traditional tools. It is not surprising, therefore, that CEOs often have been selected because they are the smartest people in the room. Organizations choose great thinkers as leaders in the same way that patients choose great diagnosticians as doctors; in both cases, little emphasis is given to bedside manner. Business school executive programs have reinforced the emphasis on cognitive leaders by focusing on case histories and the mastery of strategic and analytical competencies.

As important as the head is to leadership, it is insufficient for the demands leaders face today. The inability to exhibit compassion and display character, for instance, alienates many employees and causes them to disengage, sometimes executing a great strategy but in an uninspired way that lacks creativity and fails to generate commitment. The lack of guts may mean that a leader cannot make tough but necessary decisions regarding everything from people to product lines, which inadvertently creates a culture that is rife with indecision and lacks energy and passion.

Despite the fact that most organizations continue to emphasize the head over heart and guts, we have known for a long time that effective leaders need more than a quick mind and strong analytics. Research over the past several decades has shown this time and time again. In the nineties psychologist Bob Hogan reviewed all of the leadership research to date and concluded that personal characteristics have a strong connection to leadership effectiveness (Hogan, Curphy, & Hogan, 1994). Among the qualities that distinguish the best leaders from others are emotional maturity, the capacity to create trust, and the flexibility to work with a range of different types of people. In other words, the best leaders have heart, in addition to their other strengths. Effective leaders show tenacity, persistence, and the ability to overcome obstacles that get in their way—what we would refer to as guts.

Here are some of the other things we know from the study of leadership:

- Ask people what they want in their leaders, and they come up with words like *intelligence, honesty, determination,* and *aggressiveness,* as well as the ability to get along with people—qualities that fall neatly into our view of head, heart, and guts.

- The way people are perceived as leaders relates not only to how smart they are but to other qualities as well. People are more likely to be perceived as leaders if they have the right combination of what we're calling head, heart, and guts.

- Leaders are more likely to derail if they are untrustworthy, overcontrolling, and unwilling to make tough people and business decisions, and if they tend to micromanage their people. In other words, people *without* head, heart, and guts have a greater likelihood of derailing than those who do have these qualities.

So the idea that leaders must be able to reach beyond their cognitive ability to demonstrate other capabilities is well documented, even if it isn't practiced as frequently as it should be. Of course, a leader who relies primarily on heart or guts is equally ineffective. Most people who achieve senior-level leadership positions in business today, however, are head-oriented individuals; the heart- or guts-oriented managers tend to be stigmatized or eliminated before they make it to a top position, or they are relegated to a function best-suited to their orientation (that is, heart leaders historically have been shuttled off to staff or HR positions in "support" roles).

Integrating head, heart, and guts into leadership is both art and science. Later, we will look at what this integration entails, but first we would like to make the case for why whole leadership is so critical today.

## Factors Driving This Leadership Trend

We have seen a surprisingly large number of very smart and extremely savvy CEOs fail spectacularly in recent years. Dirk Jagger at Procter & Gamble, Mike Miles at Philip Morris, and Phil Purcell at Morgan Stanley were all extremely intelligent, smart individuals. (And they were honest ones.) Though some of their failures resulted from events beyond their control, many can be traced back to the CEOs' singled-minded approach to leadership. As driven and determined as they were, their lack of empathy, courage, instinct, and willingness to acknowledge their own vulnerability derailed them and, in some cases, their organizations.

In the past, they most likely would not have derailed. Until relatively recently, partial leaders could not only survive; they could thrive. Before world markets became more transparent, virtual, and volatile, one-dimensional leadership often sufficed. It was not unusual to find senior executives who ran companies through command and control. Conservative CEOs who eschewed risk were more the rule than the exception, and leaders who empathized and emoted were deemed "soft."

Things have changed. Specifically, some of the drivers of the change to whole leadership that we have observed are:

## Global Interdependence

In an article titled, "The Upwardly Global MBA," Nigel Andrews and Laura D'Andrea Tyson report the results of a survey of one hundred global leaders about what young executives need to succeed today. Andrews is a governor and Tyson is the dean of the London Business School, and their survey was prompted by their concern that they were not teaching MBAs what they needed to learn in order to be effective in a global marketplace. According to survey results, their concern was justified. Global executives believed that their focus on content—on teaching students what they needed to know—was insufficient. Andrews and Tyson reported that future global leaders will also need what they term "skills and attributes" as well as knowledge. These skills and attributes include the skills of giving feedback, listening, and observing. Global companies need leaders and managers who thrive on change and whose actions reflect the highest level of integrity (attributes). Many of the qualities they describe translate into heart and guts, as well as a "broader-minded" head.

Their insights apply, especially when you consider the implications of running or working in a global enterprise. First, an interpersonal orientation toward business is prevalent in most countries outside the United States. The character and personality of leaders count for as much as the products and services they sell. If you do business with other countries, you must display certain qualities (respect, humility, trust) that leaders of foreign companies unconsciously expect and value. Heart, therefore, is a critical attribute.

Second, if you are operating globally, the risks are naturally greater than if you are a domestic organization. The complexity and ambiguity involved in international transactions or working in a different culture are significant, and they require making decisions without the usual degree of certainty that they are the right ones experienced in a familiar home environment. The best global leaders are comfortable operating in an ambiguous environment, able to make risks pay off, based as much on their instinct and relationships as their analytical skills. The volatility of social, economic, and political conditions in a global marketplace demands leaders who can live with and even capitalize on this volatility. Leaders who become risk-averse in the face of uncertainty and changing conditions do not make effective global leaders.

Third, the global senior leader cannot be focused just on technical issues operations and strategy. People in leadership positions with global companies fail when they are limited to their areas of specialization. When American business executives dine with European leaders, for instance, their point of view and understanding must not only be informed on business issues, but encompass social, political, and economic trends as well. These leaders must also be open-minded and able to appreciate diverse cultural values and patterns of behavior.

## Increased Complexity of Execution

A widely held myth is that people who "get things done" in organizations operate primarily out of their heads, that they are no-nonsense, hard-driving automatons who drive and measure everything in order to achieve stellar results. Although execution does require drive and focus, Larry Bossidy and Ram Charan have provided ample evidence that execution also involves strong people skills and a willingness to roll the dice. In their books, *Execution* and *Confronting Reality*, they make it clear that emotional intelligence plays a significant role in getting things done, that the ability to encourage others to accomplish tasks is essential. They also examine courage as a quality of people who accomplish ambitious objectives, noting that pulling the trigger on tough issues requires more than a little courage.

The gestalt of execution is more complicated today than it was years ago. In the past when power was more centralized, CEOs and other organizational leaders could issue directives and expect them to be implemented with speed and diligence. Similarly, the environment in the past was less dominated with global companies, constant technological change, and other potential obstacles to accomplishing objectives. Today, execution often requires a mixture of power and influence, of risk and analysis, of explanation (or winning people's minds), and of inspiration (or winning their hearts).

## Growth

Growth requires more than a good strategy these days. As astute as a strategy might be or as attuned to customer insights and market trends, it rarely succeeds on its strategic merits alone. An imposed strategy is one that may be implemented with efficiency but not with enthusiasm, energy, innovation, or effectiveness. It is incumbent on leaders to get people excited about a growth strategy, to convince them to believe in leadership's vision for the future of the company, and to feel that they will be able to contribute to the realization of that vision. People who work for organizations are much better informed than ever before through the Internet, shorter job tenure, and continuous e-mail exchange; they are also more cynical and less trusting. They will not provide the commitment, extra effort, and innovative thinking that a commitment to growth requires unless they believe in the vision, and it is up to leaders to help create this belief and commitment.

Growth is also about risk. Few companies have the luxury in the twenty-first century of competitive advantage through superior products, market control, or pricing power, and very few sure things exist when it comes to expansion strategies. While companies may launch an acquisition or introduce a new product with confidence, they also are taking risks with every growth initiative. Conservative leadership may avoid such initiatives, knowing that the odds of success are worse than they were ten years ago; they may prefer strategies that offer much less growth and much less risk. Stagnation is a real threat to companies that adopt this mind-set, making it imperative that leaders are willing to support and implement growth strategies they truly believe in.

## Need for Innovation

*Creativity* has been defined as a unique perspective on a situation that yields a better solution. *Innovation* has been defined as driving this unique perspective through an organization and changing the way the organization performs. The former may have been fine years ago, but the latter definition is the one leaders must embrace today. Creative leaders who use their heads and who come up with better solutions are fine, but they often find their creativity has little impact on how a company performs.

Companies today are filled with breakthrough ideas that often break apart as they move through the process from origination to implementation. They become nothing more than brief, bright lightning bolts thrown into the darkness. More prosaically, they fail to do anything more than create initial excitement about a promising new product, service, process, or policy and then dissipate among unmet expectations.

The challenge today is to create a climate of innovation, and this cannot be done unless both heart and guts leadership are combined with head leadership. Knowledge management systems are of little value without accurate and open knowledge exchanges that cross internal boundaries. In many companies, people keep good ideas to themselves, fearful of sharing their creative work for fear they won't receive credit or can't control their implementation. Some people remain reluctant to share ideas with people in other functions or offices or at levels different from their own, because they have poor relationships or don't trust others to protect the ideas and use them wisely.

Companies today are seeking leaders who can create environments where people are not inhibited by fears and concerns, where they are eager, not only to share their own point of view but are receptive to hearing and integrating the ideas of others, even from sources outside their own companies. Companies are also seeking leaders who can impose discipline on the process of idea-generation. Frequently, in a misguided search for innovation, leaders embrace all new ideas, fearful that rejection will dissuade people from contributing. Or the ideas generated by those with position and authority are favored over those developed through systematic discovery. It takes guts to kill ideas that deserve to be killed, to drive truly useful new approaches to the next level and reject those lacking in potential. By the same token, leaders also need the courage to tolerate reasonable failure and to learn from their mistakes. Some terrific ideas end up failing, and leaders must communicate that a certain amount of failure comes with the innovation territory.

## Rising Expectations

Most employees expect more than a one-dimensional leader. As people working in companies become much more sophisticated and more aware of leadership and development issues through the traditional media and the Internet and dialogue with colleagues and friends, employees set higher standards for their leaders. As recently as a decade ago, the majority of the white-collar employee population was largely quiescent. They expected to be paid a modest salary, receive standard benefits, and keep their job for years, as long as they did what they were supposed to do. Few expected to be coached or developed; fewer still expected their leaders to understand them, to be intuitive, to create energy, or to break down barriers and facilitate the flow of information.

Today, largely due to the Internet and other technologies, employees are much more informed and expect much more than directions and decisions. They want to know why things happen. They expect intelligence or competence in their leaders. They realize that leadership decisions can directly affect their bonuses, raises, and the job they may or may not have tomorrow; they have witnessed seemingly invincible corporations fail because their leaders were myopic, detached, or dishonest. As a result, they seek to work for leaders who have a broader range of abilities than in the past.

Just as important, they desire leaders who can navigate in an environment of danger and unpredictability. Once-indomitable industries such as pharmaceuticals, financial services, and consumer goods that have enjoyed years of growth and profitability are suddenly threatened by new competitors, new regulations, and new technologies. Terrorism, security, hurricanes, natural disasters, and energy shortages add to the competitive challenge for all companies. It can be scary everywhere you look, and people need leaders they can trust to help them move forward. Employees naturally feel more vulnerable than ever before, which is why they expect leaders to be more than brilliant strategists; they look to their leaders to help protect them, to inform them, and to have the strength of character to do the right thing.

## Anatomy of a Whole Leader

Who are the whole leaders of today? They are all around us. When we think of a whole leader, former New York City mayor Rudy Giuliani immediately comes to mind. After 9/11, he displayed a remarkable combination of head, heart, and guts—remarkable in large part because the heart side of his leadership personality had rarely emerged in the past. He was known as tough and smart, but if anything, he was also viewed as a bit heartless because of his unrelenting crackdown on crime, his well-publicized divorce proceedings, and his relentless ambition.

In the glare of publicity following the terrorist attack, however, Giuliani displayed his emotional connectedness and vulnerability to the world. Not only was he omnipresent at the scene of the crime, lending support to firemen and families of victims, but his press conferences demonstrated and elicited genuine compassion and real feeling. When one reporter asked him about how high the casualty count might go, he responded, "When we get the final number, it will be more than we can bear." He also displayed courage and took risks in his response to the tragedy; he limited traffic into and out of New York, even though this inconvenienced millions and irritated businesses. He was willing to say, "I don't know" on numerous occasions—often considered a risky approach for a leader who wants to be viewed in command of a situation.

Though Giuliani is smart and consistently demonstrated his ability to analyze and think clearly about the problems he faced, he did not use his head in the narrow way of some leaders. He was open-minded and honest in his responses to the media; he did not show the coldly analytical, dispassionate prosecutor he once was. Neither did Giuliani obfuscate or generalize, as many politicians do in response to tough questions; nor was he defensive. He mixed stories with data and timely information with his personal interpretation of it, thus communicating insights rare for politicians.

On the business side, Andrea Jung, CEO of Avon, represents a leader who adroitly combines head, heart, and guts, and we know her well. Years ago when Avon was in a turnaround mode, Jung's strategic ability was critical; she had to develop a market strategy and build a sound business plan to restore a moribund company's fortunes. When she and her team came up with a strategy—one designed to move a traditionally people-oriented company toward a performance mind-set—Andrea Jung, as CEO, was an astute risk taker, investing in edgy advertising, shedding unprofitable brands, closing some factories, and taking other steps to invigorate performance. At the same time, people steeped in the Avon culture would never have bought into her strategy unless she was someone they could trust. Her emphasis on communicating and building relationships, as well as her insistence that everyone on her team must possess and demonstrate emotional intelligence, has fostered this trust. Over the years, Andrea has had to make tough people decisions, and she has been able to maintain the loyalty and respect of Avon employees, despite letting veteran staff go. Making these decisions required guts, and keeping morale up after making them required heart.

## Context Leadership

In both examples, you may have noticed that Jung and Giuliani responded situationally. They were able to draw on head, heart, or gut behaviors as events demanded. It helps to consider this leadership flexibility from a "context-versus-content" perspective.

We (Mercer Delta) recently conducted a content-versus-context leadership study of CEOs and discovered that context leaders were three times more effective than content leaders. Content leaders are classic head types, feeling compelled to draw on their knowledge to add value when they meet with others. Context leaders, on the other hand, add value by recognizing other resources when they enter a room and use them effectively. Operating within a context requires heart and guts; these leaders need to take the risk of depending on others to add value, and they must connect with other people so that they are willing to help them accomplish their objectives. Bill Weldon at Johnson & Johnson, Jeff Immelt at General Electric, and Steve Reinemund at Pepsi are all CEOs who practice context leadership. It is less important to them to be seen as the cleverest person around, than to be able to use their head, heart, and guts as the situation requires.

For any leader operating in a global environment, context is crucial. In the past, leaders could rely on their knowledge to solve most problems and deal effectively with most situations. Most of the time, they were operating within a relatively narrow, relatively constant environment or set of specialties. Today, the context is constantly shifting. One day, it may be important for a CEO to show compassion in announcing a divestiture or plant closing. The next day he may focus on forging an alliance with a Chinese or Asian partner to create great opportunity for growth. In both situations, the CEO must decide on a course of action, knowing that at almost every decision point the upside has a downside and that the ability to make the right decision, based solely on analysis of existing information, is virtually impossible. He must possess an almost instinctive sense of risk to determine whether venture or cost cutting is worth it. On a third day, he may face litigation due to intellectual property, shareholder, or employee claims, and to minimize the damage any of these might do, he may need to display equal parts of head, heart, and guts to manage the issues that arise.

The type of leader we are describing is not perfect or without weaknesses. She may err on the side of guts when she should rely on her intelligence. She may also naturally possess more heart than head or guts and need to be highly conscious of all facets of her leadership persona; she may need to make more of an effort to draw from these other two parts of herself that don't surface as easily as her empathy, ability to communicate, and skill at listening. The key, therefore, is maintaining access to all three parts of our leadership repertoire. Too often, leaders reflexively rely on their proven way of solving problems, approaching relationships, or capitalizing on opportunities—capabilities and qualities that have worked for them in the past. They rely too much on their past experience and automatically assume they can approach their challenges the way they always have. They end up being partial leaders, which, as we will see, can create difficult problems for their careers and their companies.

## The Problem with Partial Effectiveness

We do not want to convey the impression that partial leaders are incapable of succeeding. We have worked with many brilliant senior executives who have led teams that formulated and implemented highly profitable strategies. Smart people can often come up with innovative ideas that result in successful products and services. They can analyze data, devise partnerships and alliances, and use raw brainpower in a hundred different ways to lead their organizations.

Sometimes the context dictates head leadership. For example, companies may be market leaders that (for the moment, at least) need a CEO who is a strong strategic thinker and is astute financially. Or it may be that the situation dictates another type of partial leadership. Not-for-profits, for instance, used to be run by heart-focused CEOs because they strived to be people-oriented companies first and money-making companies second, with the result that fundraising and other expenses went up and credibility went down. If situations never changed, partial leadership would be fine. As we all know, however, things change faster than we could ever have imagined.

Because our current environment is rife with change and complex demands, the partial approach exposes a leader's Achilles' heel. When people are weak in one or two of the three areas of whole leadership, they eventually end up in situations where they lack the range of options to deal with their challenges effectively. Studies of leadership support this view. Shelley Kirkpatrick and Ed Locke found that effective leaders had a strong IQ and knowledge of their businesses (head), operated with integrity and trust (heart), and showed tenacity and drive (guts).

Let us look at some of the repercussions when people lead primarily with their cognitive strengths or analytical ability—essentially, with their heads. Specifically, here's what happens when CEOs do the following:

• *Intimidate people with their intellect.* Intellectual brilliance minus people skills or courage translates into a cold, blinding brilliance and fosters an organizational culture that replicates the leader's personality. We know one CEO who had an intimidating ability to summon up obscure data or year-old conversations in a snap second. When his direct reports disagreed with him, he overwhelmed them with statistics.

The CEO's inability to listen actively or to manage his arrogance eventually caused his management team to defer to his analysis on all occasions. No one challenged him, and as long as the company was performing, holding market share, and keeping competitors from gaining a strategic advantage, things went well. When the economy entered into recession after 9/11, and foreign competitors introduced superior technology, this CEO was unable to mobilize his team to act urgently and to take the actions that he had determined were required. Not only did he lose many of his top people, but he was unable to inspire the company to support his turnaround strategy, as astute as it might have been.

• *Confuse matters by complicating issues.* People who lead only from the head run the risk of overthinking problems and overanalyzing opportunities. Rather than outlining options clearly or providing just enough data to make a decision, they believe any problem is a set of intellectual challenges, and consequently they overwhelm everyone with statistics, ideas, and alternatives. They may lack the guts to confront the emotional dynamics of the situation or delay in making a decision. Their complex approach causes people to question their own simpler (and often more effective) ideas, and they defer to complexity.

• *Dominate conversations.* No doubt, you have encountered executives who are in love with the sound of their own voice. They perorate and pontificate. They relish displaying their vast knowledge and insights. They lack the courage to allow others to voice their opinions (they fear being proved wrong) and the heart to empathize and recognize the value others might contribute. These leaders may be extremely eloquent and convincing, but ultimately they discourage their direct reports from sharing their true feelings or ideas. The dominating leader gives the illusion of being all-controlling and all-knowing, but this illusion often ends up harming enterprises that are making decisions based on incomplete information at the top or one individual's narrow perspective.

• *Change direction without being transparent.* This leader is so smart and operates so much within his own head that people don't realize it when he has shifted strategy. He isn't aware that others are lost; he doesn't see that he is going left and they are going right. He misses the important cues embedded in the culture, some of which are due to his own action or inaction. A heart leader can read people well and sense when they are out of step, but people who lead entirely with their heads often possess little insight into others.

Ultimately, when a leader and his team don't pull together, mistakes pile up.

• *Fail to connect other people's experience to the direction in which the company is headed.* In some situations, the leader's problem is an inability to get other people to embrace a shift in policy or strategy. Leaders may do a great job explaining the new direction but are unable to inspire people to embrace the change. They cannot make the case for how the new direction will affect other people positively. They fail to discern how different individuals are responding—for example, how a vice president could really be concerned about the impact the new direction will have on his organization, resources, or empire, or how another believes it will require him to do things he had never done before, or how a third person may be plugging into previous experience that is only marginally relevant. As a result, people's embrace of the new direction is half-hearted because the reasons for their resistance are not understood.

• *Drive for performance without incorporating other values.* A results-only mentality is an anachronism. Organizations run by people with a performance-at-any-cost mentality tend to create a cynical workforce. As difficult as it is to balance an emphasis on results with values such as honesty, compassion, and trust, whole leaders make a conscious and transparent effort to do so. Even if they are not completely successful, they convey that this balance is important to them, and the result is an environment where people feel respected and where being a good team member or associate over time matters. They still drive for strong results but not to the point that nothing else matters. At best, results-obsessed organizations tend to be unpleasant places in which to work. At worst, they become the Enrons of the world.

• *Fail to create and staff a leadership pipeline.* We have saved one of the worst problems of partial leadership for last. Head-only leaders tend to be so cognitively driven that they don't understand how to successfully recruit and develop other leaders. Sometimes, their head combines with their arrogance to convince themselves they are invincible. Family dynasties and insular old-boy networks are particularly susceptible to this. Leaders in these contexts are sometimes so arrogant that they believe they will lead forever. When they are forced out or quit, however, they have not prepared anyone to take their place. The lack of successor can be devastating to companies, especially if this head-only leader departs during a crisis, and it explains why so many CEO successions in the last few years have required boards to launch a highly visible outside search.

In some cases, a company can thrive under this type of CEO's leadership, but when he leaves, the company collapses; senior leaders have not been groomed to run the organization without this dominant individual. Because his leadership was overly dependent on his analytical skills, individual judgment, and dominant personality, his absence creates a vacuum that takes time for others to fill; it can't happen suddenly.

## Does Your Organization Lean Toward Whole or Partial Leadership?

Admittedly, the question posed in this heading is difficult to answer. All organizations have a mixture of both types of leaders. Still, an alarming number of companies don't realize how many partial leaders they have in place, especially in key leadership positions. To help you diagnose what type of leaders your organization has, think about the following questions:

1. What percentage of people in leadership positions would you categorize as "the smartest person in the room"?

2. Does your company factor heart and guts criteria into the recruiting process? Do they look for people who meet a particular set of cognitive competencies, or do they go beyond the specs to consider a broader range of attributes, demonstrated across a variety of contexts?

3. Does the performance review process within your organization incorporate heart and guts criteria?

4. Is your executive development process focused exclusively on skills and knowledge acquisition, or does it give equal weight to developing people skills, risk-taking ability, and emotional intelligence acquired through experiences, mentoring, key relationships, and acknowledgment of failure?

5. What adjectives are usually used to describe your CEO? Are the words usually "brilliant, great strategist, highly analytical, results-focused, detail-oriented" or are they "well-rounded, hard-nosed but compassionate, results-focused and caring, high emotional intelligence, brave"?

6. Looking at your top leadership level, what traits do the majority of people share? Are they head traits, heart traits, guts traits, or all three?

7. Would you categorize your culture as being primarily head, heart, or guts? Does one of these traits dominate, or is it more of a mixture of two or three traits?

8. If someone asked you how you got to be CEO in your organization, would you advise him to (1) demonstrate an ability to take risks that pay off, (2) create bonds of trust with your people, (3) be a highly effective strategist? Or all three?

9. Does your company ever ask what is the right mix of head, heart, and guts required to meet the requirements of your culture and future business challenges?

◆  ◆  ◆

If your answers to these questions indicate a propensity for partial leadership, the following chapter will help you understand how development processes cause it to be ingrained. Fortunately, we also suggest ways in which development can push companies in the direction of whole leadership.

# 2

# DEVELOPING LEADERS
# THE SYSTEMIC, INTEGRATED WAY

We now possess the knowledge and the tools to develop whole leaders. Unfortunately, most companies still develop their leaders in roughly the same way they did years ago, when the demands of leadership were different. Astonishingly, a significant percentage of corporations adopt a Darwinian approach to leadership development: survivors rule. Or they occasionally throw money at leadership development through traditional classroom training or business schools, focusing almost exclusively on cognitive learning and insight. Although more companies than in the past recognize the importance of selecting, assessing, and developing emotionally intelligent leaders (and make sincere efforts to do so), these efforts are not always effective and are rarely integrated with head and guts skills.

Perhaps even more problematically, deep and systemic organization issues often prevent the best-laid plans of leadership development from coming to fruition. When a disconnect exists between targeted competencies and cultural norms, the leadership lessons won't stick. A leader may experience a transformation during the development process and come back to his organization, only to find that the culture doesn't support his transformed persona. He may have made a breakthrough during a development program in terms of speaking his mind, but when he comes back to work, colleagues and supervisors give him so much grief about his newfound honesty that he retreats to his old behaviors.

The good news is that these obstacles can be overcome with the right development approach and the commitment and involvement of an organization's executive committee. To understand how to overcome the inevitable obstacles, we first need to place these development issues in a historical context.

## Moving from the Classroom to Rocks-and-Ropes—and Beyond

Until relatively recently, the "agricultural" model of education—putting people in a classroom and force-feeding them ideas and facts—was the norm in organizations. To help people develop into good executives, an imported professor lectured about leadership and assigned case histories for people to analyze, discuss, and absorb.

The areas of cognitive study for leaders have certainly broadened over the years, encompassing everything from innovation to global management to growth strategies. The methods of teaching these cognitive subjects, however, have remained relatively constant. Case studies and lectures remain a cornerstone of the cognitive development method, and the assumption is that a solid base of knowledge in a given area greatly increases the odds of gaining mastery of this area.

Although the movement to develop leaders emotionally originated in the fifties and sixties with T-groups (sessions designed to help people get in touch with their feelings and improve interpersonal skills through open dialogue and feedback from others), it has usually remained subordinated to and segregated from the cognitive approach. One popular emotional development process in recent years has involved off-site experiences in foreign environments—both literally and figuratively foreign. People are ensconced in everything from mountain resorts to lodges to rainforests in developing countries while facilitators help them work on whatever problems are holding them back in the workplace—a bad temper, avoidance of conflict, and so on. As good as some of these off-site programs are, participants often find that the changes that occur off-site don't translate to on-site. They experience "breakthroughs" and great insights about themselves during the sessions and feel they have made positive changes because of the experience. When they return to the workplace, though, they find they revert to their old way of doing things, in large part because the organizational culture supports their old leadership style and not their new and improved ones.

Nonetheless, large corporations view these off-site retreats as important symbols of investment in leadership development, as well as excellent vehicles with which to instill desired values and traits in their leaders. For instance, UBS—a highly successful global bank we work closely with—has identified trust as a key variable in accelerating cross-business-unit working relationships to better serve their clients and execute a "one bank" strategy. Most banks today have a similar strategy and similar requirements, but UBS is in the forefront of executing their client service model because they directly acknowledge the importance of internal trust. UBS has been an innovator in developing their executives and has recently been cited by Hewitt as the number-one leadership development company. Recently, they gathered their five hundred key leaders high in the Alps to discuss the issue of trust, experience it through climbing and working together, and (this is just as important) playing together. They also listened to Wynton Marsalis demonstrate and teach that playing jazz requires a group to have both a strategy (the music) and trust (the capacity to improvise on the spot).

In terms of guts, very little has been done from a leadership development perspective, but it is receiving increasing focus and attention as a key leadership factor. While outdoor, adventure-type programs (known as rocks-and-ropes courses) have been with us for a while, they suffer from some of the same problems as emotionally based development programs. River rafting, rope-bridge crossing, battling it out in paint-ball competitions, and race-car driving may give people the chance to take some controlled risks and function as a team to meet tough challenges, but they don't directly translate back into new behaviors in office settings beyond shared memories and a new knowledge of each other. It is one thing to take a physical risk in a foreign environment and quite another to take a tough stand on a key strategic issue with a company's fortunes at stake or to sit down with a colleague you've worked with for years and tell him his performance isn't measuring up.

Though we may have evolved from a pure classroom approach, we have not evolved very far. Academicians like Laura Tyson and Henry Mintzberg have indeed argued for a more integrated approach to leadership, but little has been done in this regard in corporate settings. Even if companies recognize the need for whole leadership, they often can't develop it in an integrative manner. They may have one course that is cognitively focused and another that is interpersonally focused, but the two don't meet, and it is up to the learner to make the integration. No effort is made to help executives combine the use of their minds, their interpersonal skills, and their risk-taking ability to achieve meaningful business goals. To be an effective global leader today, understanding global market trends, or pricing, or competitors is a necessary-but-insufficient requirement for effectiveness. Being aware of one's own culture, seeing the impact of one's culture on one's perception, and understanding how culture affects the values and outlook of others are also needed for global work.

But global leaders cannot be effective if they simply adapt. They must also have their own point of view, understand their own values, and have the courage of their convictions. To deal with any particular global or international challenge, such as negotiating, making decisions, and communicating, leaders must integrate all three qualities; they must be able to display courage, brains, and emotional intelligence when confronting complex, cross-cultural, paradoxical situations.

Unfortunately, leadership development programs largely fail to help people learn how to integrate these three frameworks.

Academia and organizational processes have reinforced a segregated approach. If you examine any business school syllabus in the United States or in Europe, you'll find courses centered on "technical" material: finance, marketing, and so on. One or two courses may have an emotional or risk-taking component ("Developing the International Executive," for instance), but the focus is largely cognitive.

Similarly, the hiring and the rewards-and-recognitions processes emphasize cognitive development. Typically, the best students from the best schools are hired at the largest, most successful companies. Many organizations hire junior people based on grades and quality of schools attended, and they select more experienced applicants based on their track record and ability to meet the job specs. If a global leadership position opens up, for instance, the key assignment criteria include a list of typical head competencies: a clear grasp of business strategies and priorities, an understanding of the competitive superiority of products and services, and a track record of success in one's area of functional expertise. In most cases, heart and guts skills such as an ability to adjust to the local culture, being able to adapt products and services to local markets, and an ability to supervise, motivate and develop local employees are not included in the assignment criteria.

Companies use the same approach to rewards and recognitions. Meeting or exceeding performance-based objectives and delivering measurable results are usually the main criteria. People who receive the largest bonuses and the choicest of promotions are those who deliver the best results. Only recently have some companies striven to adapt the General Electric approach of focusing not only on results but on how those results were achieved. In some cases, succession-planning discussions are broadening to include discussion of intangible qualities such as empathy, emotional intelligence, and even compassion.

Mostly, the measurement of tangible, concrete accomplishments governs both the hiring and the rewards-and-recognitions systems. It is far easier to measure whether a manager's team has met a revenue target, for instance, than whether that manager has built an aligned team or created a culture of trust and accountability. As a result, these systems push leadership development in a cognitive direction, since all these measurable qualities are head-based.

## Creating a Risk-Taking, Interpersonal, Intelligent Development Process

Most companies are influenced by the factors just discussed, but they do not have to be constrained by them. As the world becomes increasingly complex and volatile, a greater need exists for leaders who can move beyond cold analysis and strategic execution. Without senior executives whom the majority of employees can trust and connect with, cynicism and disengagement follow. Without leaders who can seize opportunities when they appear, such as acquiring another company, discounting prices when a competitor is weakened, or shedding nonperforming assets in advance of a recession, large companies gradually become slow and ineffective. The rationale clearly exists for companies to take the four steps discussed next.

### Step 1: Address Systemic Issues

First, *take care of the systemic issues before implementing a development process*. This first step is absolutely critical for whole leadership development, and it is nearly always neglected. In fact, leadership development is often used to cure systemic ills—an approach that never works. For instance, a company wants more innovative leaders, so they design the development process to help people exhibit competencies associated with innovation. After going through development, these individuals may indeed think out of the box, and they may have mastered techniques to catalyze innovative behavior in others. When they attempt to put these techniques into practice, though, they are stymied by systemic issues. They may find a culture that is averse to the kind of risk taking that is required to drive innovation. As a result, when these innovative leaders attempt to turn a breakthrough idea into a new product or service, they are met with resistance at all levels. They hear excuses like "this will cost too much," or "it will require the active participation of too many key people," or "the project is badly timed," or "it is off-strategy." After seeing their attempts to be more innovative shot down two or three times, these leaders are discouraged and fall back on their old, less-innovative behaviors.

In fact, when companies fail to address systemic issues in advance, development programs can have a negative impact on the organization. For instance, we know of a company that has been emphasizing collaborative skills in its training. Managers emerge from the training excited about crossing functions and other boundaries in order to exchange information and ideas. When they attempt to do so, however, they are discouraged in their efforts. For example, the senior executive team, which remains internally competitive because of succession hopes, withholds information and reinforces a silo mentality. On one level, they recognize that true collaboration across boundaries will spur innovation. When it comes to implementation, however, the head of Operations resists involving a Finance leader in reviewing how he can improve his strategic sourcing, and the Finance leader won't work closely with the head of Engineering to develop the right metrics to track product development costs across business units. These implicit attitudes and behaviors create tremendous frustration and cynicism among people who receive the message through their development programs that collaboration is important. They conclude that their leadership is insincere and hypocritical, and this belief erodes whatever gain the leadership development program achieves. In this case, the company would have been better off never having launched the development program.

Organizational development must be implemented together with leadership development. We frequently use the congruence model as a way of understanding how systemic issues affect leadership behavior. This approach focuses on how the formal and informal organizations affect work and output. As we see it, understanding the informal organization before designing leadership development interventions can help surface systemic roadblocks. Companies must address the obstacles that make it difficult for leaders to exhibit heart and guts behaviors or to think in ways that run counter to the culture. If the organization is historically conservative, and its processes and policies mitigate against taking chances, these processes and policies must be changed. Only then can leadership development help people learn to take educated risks and translate this learning into job behaviors.

For example, we recently conducted a senior executive program for a global company. The focus of the program was on leadership actions that could create organic growth. During the day, the program addressed the actions leaders could take to foster, measure, drive, and capture sources of growth in their business units. In the evening, over drinks, we asked the participants to write down the "unwritten rules" of the company on a note card and submit as many as they wished. The unwritten rules included "don't challenge the boss" and "always drive your PowerPoint by each executive committee member before asking their endorsement as a team." Many of them were innocuous, even fun, but many directly conveyed important messages about the company's culture. Only by uncovering these systemic issues could real learning proceed.

## Step 2: Involve the Executive Committee

Next, *make sure the executive committee is involved in and supportive of the development process.* This means more than token involvement or oversight responsibility. When executive committees are not involved and aligned (and they often are not), the process goes awry. The biggest problem, as just outlined, is that people are developed in a way that's independent of systemic issues. When a CEO and his team are not part of the process, leadership development becomes something it was never intended to be.

For instance, a large, global company has been experiencing problems related to trust. Because of the fiercely competitive and highly politicized culture of the company, animosities have existed between different functions and among different players for years. As this company becomes increasingly reliant on a matrix structure of organization—interdependent teams and alliances—the pervasive distrust is slowing things down and eroding accountability. A new executive team, therefore, wants to increase trust throughout

the company, and they have empowered the leadership development group to implement training designed to achieve this goal. A
sophisticated and multidimensional trust-building component is
built into their leadership development program, and hundreds of
leaders go through it. When they return to their jobs, however, the
tensions between functions and among different hierarchical levels
are still as strong as ever. When the "developed" individuals
attempt to extend trust to others, they often are burned. Thus they
revert to their old, distrustful ways, and, if anything, the culture has
been further diminished. The vice president in charge of leadership
development and the outside consultants who work with him are
aware of these failures, but they feel powerless to remedy them since
the executive team shows no interest in getting involved or changing the organization in ways that will support the leadership development efforts.

We were recently engaged by another large Fortune 500 company to design a senior leadership meeting focusing on execution.
The goal of the meeting was to identify the challenges of execution
within this organization, surface them, and resolve them. We
designed and facilitated the meeting, and as it unfolded, the dialogue clearly began to surface the issues. The next step, however,
did not occur: the senior team could not come to terms with their
own role in creating the issues. The preferred solution was to "fix"
things through more training, awareness, and rewards, and through
punishment of those outside the room.

Development doesn't take place in a vacuum. It often requires
parallel organizational actions that, when combined with leadership
development, have a synergistic effect. When the management team
opts out of the process, however, this synergy is missing. One company we know well is a large, global, decentralized financial services
company, with strong performance through many autonomous business units. This decentralization has had many positive outcomes,
such as more opportunities to develop leaders, more decision making close to the customer, and smarter allocation of resources.

However, because the market requires more synergistic solutions developed in the "white spaces" between these business units,

company leaders naturally look upward for prioritization. No one is certain which of their agenda items could represent a significant enterprise opportunity and which is a suboptimized solution for their own business. The senior leadership team believes that to step in and set a clear direction would diminish leadership in the ranks. The leadership development effort, therefore, is geared toward helping people understand what decentralization means and learning how to partner across the company and how to lead teams effectively. This is helpful, but market and regulatory forces are now demanding that the senior team step up and enumerate their priorities. If they were part of the dialogue, as well as the development process, they might recognize that this represents leadership rather than removes it, and the development training could focus on these articulated priorities.

As you might expect, leadership development that takes place without executive participation produces partial leaders. The focus of development often becomes skewed toward one particular skill or area of knowledge; the CEO or another executive isn't there to suggest a broader, more holistic perspective on the problem. For instance, one company hoped to use leadership development to foster a growth mentality among its managers. Although the CEO was well aware that a growth mentality requires head, heart, and guts (you need to take appropriate risks and engage people in the cause, along with having a sound growth strategy), the leadership development program turned into something else entirely. The emphasis became learning how to execute well without making mistakes—a purely cognitive skill (and not the right one for growth, in any case).

## Step 3: Use Leadership Development as a Diagnostic Tool

Realistically, management is not always aware of the systemic issues that weaken a company; nor are they as concerned about those issues as they should be. The early stages of leadership development, though, can make a compelling case for management to pay attention to and do something about these issues. We conduct many Action Learning programs for global companies, and a strong component of these programs is to foster a dialogue in real time on real issues between participants and senior leaders. Action Learning is useful in creating a temporary system with unique values incorporating head, heart, and guts, in which a different type of conversation can occur. If this is done right, participants feel free to provide senior management with their feedback—honest, incisive feedback that fosters insight and illuminates problems that might not otherwise occur—at the top of the company.

More significantly, it makes "whole leader" development more feasible. When people talk about how they are afraid to speak out on an issue or how they feel their direct reports don't believe they have their best interests at heart, executive leadership becomes aware of the other dimensions of a problem—dimensions that go beyond cognitive matters. For example, when innovation is the focus of leadership development, the training often involves providing leaders with techniques to foster creative thinking among their people. With this diagnostic element, however, management is alerted that managers are convinced that the company always comes down hard on failure and that they suspect their people don't feel sufficiently comfortable to share ideas that challenge the traditions and norms of the organization. These are heart and guts issues, and they can then be incorporated into the development process.

## Step 4: Customize the Process

Finally, *customize the process for your organizational situation and incorporate head, heart, and guts dimensions into the design.* We will be talking about the development process throughout the book, but for now we want to emphasize two points. First, don't rely on trendy, off-the-shelf, or even "best practice" institutional programs. What appears cost-effective usually is not, because each culture, company, and industry is unique, and leadership is the result of systemic factors, both positive and negative, as well as competitive issues that are not transferable. You need to structure your leadership development with the strengths and weaknesses of your company in mind. When we do strategic leadership development, we always link it to a company's business context, CEO agenda, competitive challenges, history, management performance system, or something similar. We have learned through long and sometimes hard experience the difficult lesson that importing a program that works elsewhere, particularly at the top, often encounters cultural resistance.

Similarly, we evaluate the head, heart, and guts requirements of a given company. Some companies should not give equal emphasis to head, heart, and guts. A company may be facing a set of paradoxical strategic choices, requiring its leaders to make more complex decisions and eschew simple solutions. It may be facing a regulatory, environmental, or competitive crisis and must require its leaders to veer away from its traditional conservative approach; they need a more daring strategy to deal with the crisis effectively. It may also be that an organization must prepare a cadre of people for positions that will be unlike those of today, and it is incumbent on development to build a strong business case for the new behavior.

The process itself can vary considerably, depending on situational factors, but let us share with you a simple approach that we have evolved.

The first learning theme involves a presentation on whatever theme or subject the development program is designed to address. Typically, the morning session is devoted to explaining the topic— what *innovation* or *collaboration* or *global management* means, the skills required to be good at it, and examples that illustrate the points. This is the cognitive part of the program.

The second element usually takes place during the afternoon session and involves people doing exercises or receiving coaching around the personal issues that surface in a given topic area. If the theme is innovation, we might talk to participants about how innovative they feel they are, what blocks to their creativity they encounter at work, and when and why they have been innovative.

At the end of the session, they are given an assignment related to innovation (or whatever the focus might be) that they have to practice in the workplace over the next few days, weeks, or months.

Third, people test what they've learned. This practical application of what they have learned constitutes the guts phase of development. Invariably, people must test new behaviors and face new challenges, and because it is happening in a "real" (as opposed to a theoretical) environment, consequences exist. They may be embarrassed, feel awkward, place themselves in uncomfortable situations, practice skills they're not good at, and even fail. Obviously, all this requires courage.

The fourth element involves a return to the program after the passage of time. We listen to participants describe their experiences and provide them with feedback on how well (or how poorly) they integrated head, heart, and guts leadership behaviors.

## Recognizing That Different Combinations of Head, Heart, and Guts Are Needed in Different Situations

As we suggested earlier, we take into consideration a company's leadership development goals for a particular position (or particular team or group) before designing a program. Some jobs require more heart than guts; some assignments demand more head than heart. The mix of head, heart, and guts is different for a leadership team that is resizing a business than it is for a chief executive expanding into new markets. It's important to design a process with these situational requirements in mind.

In *The Leadership Pipeline* by Ram Charan, Steve Drotter, and Jim Noel, the authors make the point that as people move through different levels in an organization, they must adjust their behaviors and their value orientations accordingly. The skills and values at an individual contributor level, for instance, are quite different from those at a first-time manager level.

One change a first-time manager needs to make is to value the contributions of others rather than focus on his own performance. The authors emphasize that it is not just acquiring a new group of skills and values that is necessary, but letting go of skills and values that made the manager successful at an earlier level.

To develop people effectively, consider how head, heart, and guts manifest themselves at different organizational levels:

### Head

Level 1 (first-line supervisor): Learning technical skills

Level 2 (manager of managers): Coordinating horizontal people and projects

Level 3 (executive): Creating strategy

### Heart

Level 1: Managing one-on-one relationships

Level 2: Coaching, nurturing talent, and aligning teams

Level 3: Managing complexity, dealing with personal derailers, handling ambiguity

### Guts

Level 1: Giving tough feedback and dealing with other tough performance-management issues

Level 2: Managing conflict among units, allocating resources, taking the risk to speak up

Level 3: Making the tough calls (closing plants, redeploying assets and resources, and so on)

These descriptions of levels are clearly generalized, and you may find that you need to make adjustments based on a more detailed delineation of levels or the particular requirements in your company. Although the general development goal is to help people integrate these three types of behaviors, the more specific goal is to help them integrate the right mix of behaviors.

## Figure 2.1. The Leadership Pipeline

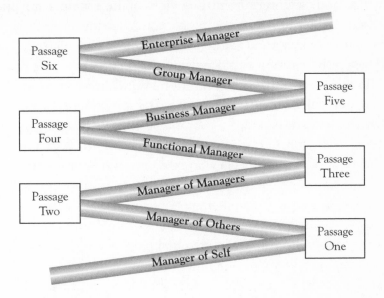

Source: Charan, R., Drotter, S., & Noel, J. (2001). *The Leadership Pipeline*. San Francisco: Jossey-Bass, p. 7. Reprinted with permission of John Wiley & Sons.

## Guts: The Trickiest Developmental Area

Admittedly, the development of guts is largely unexplored territory. In fact, we have heard more than one CEO doubt that courage can be taught. Although it is not possible to transform an inherently risk-averse individual into someone who throws caution to the winds, we have found that people can make incremental changes in their approach to taking risks. When we work with people in guts areas, we give them feedback on how they are not displaying courage (such as refusing to make tough decisions) and help them understand the negative consequences of this behavior. We also support them in their efforts to display guts; we share tools and techniques that might assist them. Many times, this approach spurs them to exhibit greater courage in the workplace in small ways.

In *The Courage to Act*, authors Merom Klein and Rod Napier emphasize that courage can be learned, especially if it is approached as behavior that exhibits the following five traits: purpose, will, rigor, risk, and candor. By being conscious of these factors and practicing the associated behaviors, people can overcome their fears and learn to take risks and do things they have never done before.

Within the business world, we have found that the same person may be risk-averse in one organization and willing to take risks in another company. In the former, the systemic messages convey that taking chances is a bad idea—that management comes down hard on anyone who takes a risk and fails. In the latter, the systemic messages are not only that people who take risks and fail won't be punished (unless they take foolish risks and keep repeating the same mistakes) but that risk-embracing people will be rewarded in various ways. Again, we come back to our earlier admonition to be aware of the systemic issues in your company before embarking on a leadership development program.

Realistically, most large bureaucracies don't want their leaders to display too much courage, no matter what is said to the contrary. Large companies, guided by concerns about litigation, shareholders, and publicity, invariably evolve toward the less-risk option. And any company beyond the early stages of the business cycle can only tolerate a certain level of rebelliousness and iconoclastic behavior. Although some organizations tolerate eccentric geniuses who speak their mind and take risks, these tend to be tokens rather than the rule. The complexity of most companies today is such that compliance is preferred to guts; it is difficult to get much done if everyone is speaking his mind or following a different drummer.

Our point is not that all leaders must show courage at every opportunity. They must learn when and how to display this courage—what Joseph Badarocco of Harvard University describes as "Defining Moments"—those infrequent leadership choice points when you truly create your character and shape your value system. Speaking up when you feel something is unfair or unethical certainly is one display of guts, but speaking up to your boss when he is eyeball deep in a crisis may not elicit the best reaction or demonstrate the best timing. Similarly, delivering an angry peroration about the company's fascist mentality and stalking out of the meeting may not be the best way to communicate courage.

Part of the development process, therefore, needs to be devoted to how and when to display guts. For instance, leadership development can help people understand that when they speak their mind, they should also make sure to listen to other people's points of view, demonstrate that they've listened, and try to persuade them to another way of thinking without going into attack mode.

◆ ◆ ◆

To make this material as accessible and user-friendly as possible, we divide the following chapters into separate head, heart, and guts sections. The next section ("Part Two: Head Leadership"), for instance, contains chapters that correspond to the key cognitive issues that are critical to leaders today ("Rethinking the Way We Do Things Around Here," "Reframing the Boundaries," "Getting Things Done," and "Developing and Articulating a Point of View"). In real business life, these topics are not distinct. For example, the next chapter (Chapter Three) is about global rethinking, but this is not just a head issue. We are putting it in the head section because rethinking is the first step that must be taken. But along with this cognitive restructuring come emotional issues, such as being empathetic with other cultures, and guts issues, such as risking a relationship with a small third-world company.

You'll find chapters, further along in the book, on integrating these head, heart, and guts behaviors. First, though, let's concentrate on the head.

# Part Two

# HEAD LEADERSHIP

# 3

# RETHINKING THE WAY WE DO THINGS AROUND HERE

Just as it has become increasingly important to rethink conventional wisdom, it has become increasingly difficult to do so. The growing complexity, volatility, and ambiguity of business and competition constantly demands new perspectives. This environment, however, is uncertain and filled with risk, and it is human nature to cleave to tried-and-true methods in unpredictable times. Faced with this paradox, many leaders opt for the latter—the traditional—course, especially in successful companies with strong cultures.

The ability to rethink is not something you find listed under leadership traits, at least in most traditional definitions of leadership. Yet like many of the traits discussed in this head section, they are becoming increasingly timely and particularly useful in a global, complex environment.

We should also add that although we're discussing this trait as part of the head, rethinking also involves the heart and guts. You need to start cognitively by rethinking standard operating procedure; you then require heart to understand the impact your rethinking will have on the people around you, and you need guts to take risks and turn this commitment into actions. For now, though, let's focus on the cognitive aspect of this trait and why it is so difficult for many leaders to get their mind around it.

## Finding a Fresh Perspective
## Is Easier Said Than Done

Most business leaders recognize that change is inevitable and that they must engage in new, innovative, and improved ways of behavior to stay ahead of the competition and deliver for the customer. This recognition, though, infrequently translates into conscious behavior or a fresh theory of the case. In the abstract, the notion of rethinking makes perfect sense, and few would disagree that it is necessary. When it comes down to specific actions with consequences, however, changing behavior, strategies, tactics, rituals, and traditions is much more difficult.

Thomas Kuhn, an expert in the history of science and author of *The Structure of Scientific Revolutions* and other books, coined the term *paradigm shift*. Kuhn found that, contrary to expectations, most scientists are not independent, objective thinkers but rather operate within their paradigms. As an example, Kuhn cites Ptolemy and his insistence that the sun revolves around the earth—an idea that was considered scientific fact for hundreds of years until Copernicus came along and rethought the conventional wisdom.

Our point is that many business leaders are like scientists, convinced that they are independent thinkers but in reality are at the mercy of the prevailing paradigm. This can result in dangerous self-deception. As Kuhn notes, "The man who is striving to solve a problem defined by existing knowledge and technique is not just looking around. He knows what he wants to achieve, and he designs his instruments and directs his thoughts accordingly."

Beyond the natural tendency to stay within the paradigm, other factors, such as the following, predispose leaders to avoid rethinking.

• *Pressure to produce results.* Intense pressure to produce results makes it difficult to find the cognitive space necessary to consider alternative approaches. Or perhaps it is more accurate to say that leaders think about the future and recognize that things will change, but these thoughts are quickly obliterated by the immediate needs of the business. An executive with a successful product that accounts for a significant amount of company revenue just can't get his mind around the idea that the product might be nearing the end of its life cycle; rather, he attributes the situation to a sluggish sales force or temporary market forces or even the weather. To dwell on the possibility of demise also means to dwell on changing the entire nature of the product mix or product portfolio, and this can be overwhelming and easily postponed. As a result, this leader will focus on driving revenue, which relieves the pressure for results temporarily. This seems to be a much better alternative than rethinking everything—a monumental task that will produce a monumental headache.

• *Need for guts.* Rethinking takes guts. Whole leaders are able to see things differently and act on what they see because of their courage. To contemplate the notion of making major changes raises all sorts of disconcerting scenarios. Just entertaining the possibility of a new business model requires a boldness that some senior executives lack. We have had conversations with business leaders who have told us they recognize the possibility that their company will be out of business in five years if they don't begin the process of change, but they lack the courage to face reality, hoping they can beat the clock or that something will turn up or that others will step forward. They can rationalize this lack of courage in many ways, including the fact that their people aren't ready for change. They are well aware of the enormous resistance people can display when a company attempts to do things differently, and rather than have to deal with this resistance, they prefer to maintain the status quo. People expect leaders to fix problems and not to ask employees to change. To avoid thwarting these expectations, leaders implement temporary fixes rather than long-term solutions that require people to make sacrifices or learn new ways of doing things.

• *Lack of time to think.* Senior executives become caught in the activity trap and don't allow themselves time to rethink. Most executives we work with today confront hundreds of e-mails daily, continuous meetings (sometimes two at once), a deluge of information over the Internet, ever-escalating demands for performance from clients and customers, and direct reports who would like more attention and coaching. In the noise, it is sometimes hard to see the imperceptible signals that things are changing; it is easy to deny them in the face of unpleasant realities. These executives are in constant motion, traveling around the globe, attending conferences on cutting-edge topics, and responding to cell phones, Blackberries, urgent pages, voice mails, and other technological prompts. Amid all this churn, they fool themselves into believing they are seeing the business in new, exciting ways. In reality, people are merely substituting hectic schedules and thinking abstractly about big new ideas for the more difficult task of thinking long and hard about how things will change and about the need to change, as well as evolving a systematic plan and process to address what's needed. Many leaders we've met don't understand the difference between having a new idea and committing themselves to implementing it.

• *Rising cost of reinvention.* Complexity is daunting. Marshalling all the forces necessary to change a business or even to implement a new program or policy can seem impossibly complex. The cost of reinvention is always going up, the timeframe for implementing a new process or program is shrinking, and competitors, by definition, are making inroads and limiting options for new strategies. Given all this, it is much easier to keep moving in the same old direction.

• *Power of rituals.* Cultural rituals are powerful. As sincere as people may be in their desire to rethink the way things are done, they are subject to the pull of company traditions and unwritten codes of conduct. Organizations that have always been run by white males with similar backgrounds may acknowledge the importance of diversity but have trouble achieving it now. Corporations that have always maintained extensive internal staff functions to analyze, synthesize, and present culturally relevant data may find it difficult to outsource payroll, billing, and other human resource and finance activities to India or China. Forsaking these norms through rethinking requires a leap of faith. Staff meetings, sales events, internal memos, monthly reports—all these and many more examples constitute corporate rituals, and for veteran executives who have been practicing these corporate rituals for years, asking for change is akin to asking an isolated tribal leader to forsake a ritual sacrifice that placates the gods. If they have adhered to this ritual for twenty years, and the gods have usually provided the rain they needed for their crops to grow, why should they give it up?

## Why Now Is a Good Time to Start Rethinking

We live and work in a time when business cycles are increasingly shorter and the need to challenge the business model is continuous. The information revolution, escalating technological capacity, the global marketplace, and myriad other factors make decision making far more challenging than in the past. Leaders today must cope with paradox, confront complex ideas, and develop an integrated worldview. Most of the tried-and-true solutions to problems are no longer viable. Most of the standard ways of capitalizing on opportunities lack necessary speed and innovation. Without the ability to rethink conventional approaches, leaders will fall behind. We see many leaders who believe that business models exist to be challenged but can't or won't create the environment for that to occur.

A brief historical perspective illuminates how critical rethinking is today. Twenty years ago when competition was based on product, most rethinking focused on whether a company should change something about the product (packaging, price, and so on). At some point in the 1980s, companies began redefining competition, not just around the products they produced but the way they delivered these products. Speed, availability, customization, and other factors began conferring competitive edge. Research and development, therefore, ceased to be the primary focus of corporate rethinking. It became necessary to take larger, systemic risks: restructuring the company for faster delivery of local resources, for instance. Systemic change of this type entails more risk and is more difficult to implement.

Nonetheless, change is absolutely essential. The most successful leaders and companies, such as GE, Johnson & Johnson, Bank of America, and many others, tend to be those that rethink who their customers are, question what business they are in, and fearlessly restructure to better serve customers. Nokia reinvented itself after existing for a hundred years as a lumber company by divesting themselves of everything but microchips and telephones. This was a massive rethinking of a historically entrenched business. IBM and EMC both transformed themselves from manufacturing into services companies. Time Warner has gone from being a magazine publisher to being an integrated media, communications, and entertainment provider. Travelers Insurance integrated with CitiBank to become the largest financial services company in the world.

Reconceptualizing of this sort, however, isn't a guarantee of success. You can rethink things the wrong way. AT&T, for instance, threw billions of dollars into the computer business and has had little to show for it. They restructured after the consent decree years ago, but they had trouble going beyond structural change. General Motors sought to become a data company and then a satellite company, acquiring and then divesting EDS and Direct TV. Sony, over the years, has acquired and divested everything from orange juice businesses to movie production studios. It is not enough, therefore, to re-imagine the organization. It has to be the right re-imagining.

Still, organizations need leaders who are willing to challenge the status quo, to consider alternatives to what has helped a company achieve enormous success in the past, and that may even be contributing to its present success. These leaders are better able to deal with the unpredictable and unnerving situations that seem to pop up daily. They have the wherewithal to approach different people in different ways; they can handle the brilliant young tech guru who is unwilling to conform to the company's norms or who demands that the company take risks it has never taken before; they are the ones who will help navigate new global initiatives, learning to work effectively in worlds where the old rules no longer apply.

This need for leaders who can rethink isn't going away. If anything, the need will intensify in the coming years, as change accelerates at an even higher rate and global initiatives move beyond

Asian and European markets and into developing countries where traditional ways of doing business don't apply.

## How to Catalyze Fresh Viewpoints

No doubt, some individuals will never be willing to shift their perspectives and re-evaluate their beliefs. For many reasons (innate conservatism, vested interest in the status quo) they refuse to consider a new way of seeing or doing. As a result, they either refuse to rethink or only pretend to do so.

The majority of executives, though, can learn to rethink. Perhaps a better way of putting this is: They can find good reasons to move past their fears and see things differently. All the obstacles to rethinking that we discussed earlier—daunting complexity, the power of paradigms, falling into the activity trap—can be overcome, given the right developmental approach. Here are some ways of doing so that we have found to be effective in both coaching and teaching executives across a variety of companies and industries.

- *Hit people with data.* A rational explanation of why it is important to see things in a fresh light rarely is successful. You can present the most convincing case possible for viewing global trends in a new light or for considering alternatives to an established process, but you will fail to penetrate outer defenses against new thoughts. People require compelling data to change their thinking. These data can be personal or marketplace-based. For example, data might take the form of feedback from direct reports that an individual's micromanagement style no longer is effective or from demographic proof that a market is migrating to a competitor. Whatever form they take, data must convey a singularly powerful message: *The way you're doing things now isn't working.* This unequivocal fact of failure, especially if the individual thought his current approach was successful, is jarring. It eliminates the rationalization that can keep people stuck on established paths. Data need to be convincing. It is not enough for one person to protest against a micromanagement style or for one questionable study on market share to be presented to a leader. The data should be unequivocal. In the face of convincing facts, denial isn't an option. Most leadership programs we conduct begin with some confrontation with reality. Often we encourage companies to bring their harshest critics (sometimes a Wall Street analyst) into the room to talk with their people to provide an external and more sobering look at the fundamentals of their business. We've found this type of wake-up call to be invaluable.

• *Encourage tolerance of ambiguity.* We were coaching a senior executive who was skilled and accomplished but was very much stuck in his ritualized behavior patterns. Though he was highly organized and ran meetings with great efficiency, he rarely used these meetings to elicit real dialogue or encourage innovative thinking and problem solving. To help him out of this rut, we asked him to start going into meetings without fixed outcomes in mind. This meant he could not list, either on paper or in his mind, goals he wanted the meeting to accomplish. We even encouraged him to try a meeting or two with no agenda, no financials, and no Power-Point. Instead, he had to tolerate the ambiguity of open-ended discussion and free-flowing ideas. He admitted this prospect terrified him, but perhaps to humor us, he made the effort. Gradually, he found that his direct reports were more willing to venture opinions, explore options, and propose ideas that were more creative and risky than in the past. His fixed idea of what constituted an effective meeting, which he had held for twenty years, began to change.

• *Break the frame of cultural traditions.* Leadership development often doesn't work because the development process replicates the culture and reinforces prevailing views. Overtly or subtly, the process prohibits information and ideas that run counter to organizational norms. Executives may sincerely want to develop a new mind-set or behaviors among key leaders, but the process implicitly fosters the same cultural assumptions that sabotage the explicit message. Creative leadership development designs, usually in some form of learning-while-doing (for example, combining business problem solving with self- and group awareness) can help break the frame of cultural traditions. Creative development can be done through a mixture of personal feedback, challenging business situations, and fresh perspectives and information; people are taken out of familiar environments and forced to rely on new ideas and ways of looking at things to solve complex business problems. When they no longer can fall back on tried-and-true methods or operate within a comfortable system, they start seeing and doing things differently. When they break frame once, they are more likely to do it again. Sometimes, this frame-breaking experience happens naturally rather than through a formal development program. An overseas assignment or even a job with a new organization can provide opportunities for reassessment and rethinking. Coaching, too, can catalyze alternative ways of viewing familiar situations. The key, though, is sustaining this rethinking past a singular experience, and formal programs such as Action Learning are good at achieving this goal; they provide the type of head, heart, and guts training that has a long-term effect.

We should add that these three methods tend to be least effective in highly successful, polite organizations where no burning platform for change exists and negative feedback is sugar-coated, that is, where politeness prevents issues from being confronted. The catalysts for rethinking—new information and ideas—are in short supply. As a result, people are encouraged to maintain their mind-sets and avoid introducing controversial or provocative concepts into the culture. In this environment, rethinking is a disconcerting idea.

Here is an example of what we mean.

Carl is a senior executive with a large package-goods corporation; he has significant strengths. He's a highly emotionally intelligent leader who advanced through HR. Over the years he has been a mentor and coach to many individuals. In recent years, though, the company's performance, measured through market share and stock price, has declined; although still highly successful, it is attempting to develop a more performance-oriented approach among its leaders. As part of this development, a coach has been working with Carl to become a more performance-oriented and innovative leader, especially when it comes to creating the type of team climate in which innovation flourishes. Unfortunately, when the coach collects feedback, most of the criticisms of Carl's management style are couched in praise, so it's difficult to discern any negatives. Everyone knows that Carl's desire to be liked sometimes gets in his way of facing conflict, meeting deadlines, and producing results, but no one in his highly civilized culture is willing to tell him that. Even Carl's boss is reluctant to level with him. As a result, Carl rejects the coach's suggestions that he has to view his team leadership differently, that he may not be doing marginal performers a favor by keeping them in place, and that his desire to be admired and included sometimes prevents him from making tough but necessary decisions. Carl is unable to rethink these issues because his culture doesn't provide the impetus for doing so.

But here's a counterexample.

Carol Bartz, the CEO of Autodesk, is brilliant at rethinking the way they do things around her company. Since becoming the company's CEO in 1992, Bartz has helped the organization rethink its core concepts more than once. When she joined the firm, which specializes in computer-aided design software, the company had one main product and a narrow market of designers and architects. Bartz immediately began expanding and diversifying, eventually reshuffling the customer base to include manufacturers, the building and construction industry, and infrastructure businesses (roads and bridges). In 1999, she took the company in a new direction, buying Discreet Logic for $410 million and acquiring technology used for Hollywood animation and special effects. In a relatively short period of time, Autodesk became a significant player in media, with Discreet products being used in movies such as *Titanic* and *Lord of the Rings* and accounting for 15 percent of Autodesk's revenue. A few years later, faced with an economic downturn, Bartz reconceptualized the company again, this time focusing on selling software by subscription, enabling customers to use software for a specific period of time, and entitling them to free upgrades during this period. This radical reconfiguration of Autodesk's business model not only produced a more predictable revenue stream, but it also resulted in a faster cycle time for producing new software.

In a *Fortune* magazine interview, Bartz described her ability to rethink this way: "I've turned this company around three times. It's like a sailboat. The weather changed, and I had to change. The economy changed, the technology changed, and luckily I had a patient board."

## Rethinking Is Relative

Perhaps leaders exist who are continuously rethinking their business, who are willing to re-examine even their most successful ideas and approaches and then toss them out in favor of new and improved concepts. In our experience, though, this type of extremely open-minded leader is unusual. Fortunately, we don't need leaders who constantly rethink the way things are. It takes a lot of guts and heart to challenge your own business model, values, or assumptions about what is true, and leaders who are able to achieve this goal will greatly enhance their effectiveness.

More significantly, leaders must learn to pick their spots for rethinking. Taken to an extreme, rethinking can become counterproductive. People view reflexive rethinkers as impulsive, fickle, or even flaky. If you are continuously coming up with a new approach every day, your team will quickly learn to seriously filter your latest idea. On the other hand, windows exist when it makes sense to see people and situations differently. The opportunity may come in a leadership development program or through coaching, which is the primary purpose of both of these endeavors. It may happen when a leader has suffered a setback and is open to new ways of doing things. It may occur when a company experiences a setback or declining performance, and the system becomes "unfrozen" or open to new thinking. Whenever these windows present themselves (and it is our experience that they do not present themselves regularly), leaders must be prepared to look through them with a fresh and concentrated gaze.

There are instances, too, when rethinking isn't necessarily the sign of a head, heart, and guts leader. We once presented direct quotes from fifteen people who indicated that a leader was pursuing the wrong strategy and who was resistant, aloof, and unable to be flexible when flexibility was critical. This leader read the quotes and immediately rejected them, insisting that they came from fifty individuals who were not in tune with his vision.

Was this guy an idiot because he ignored the evidence before him and refused to rethink his business strategy? Or was he a courageous leader who was following his instincts instead of the data and would slowly bring his resistant organization around?

Finally, we should acknowledge that many times, organizations hire consultants to do their rethinking for them. The reality is that companies are highly activity-oriented and resource-scarce, and they want to drive toward closure. They lack the time or the intellectual freedom to consider 180-degree changes from established practices. At the same time, they know they could benefit from fresh thinking. That is when they call in the consultants, who prompt and prod them in fresh directions.

We are not suggesting that organizational leaders can ignore this skill if they hire consultants. Instead, what we hope is that leaders will allow consultants to catalyze their rethinking and to introduce new elements into the culture that force companies to see things in a new light.

◆ ◆ ◆

One area that many leaders are forced to rethink is how they draw the boundaries around their role, their work, and their organization. In the next chapter we will examine the ways in which a changing world is demanding that leaders reframe the boundaries by which they have defined themselves and their roles in the world.

# 4

# REFRAMING THE BOUNDARIES

Companies are defined by boundaries. Despite a growing organizational recognition that hard-and-fast boundaries are things of the past, individuals within most organizations still fail to think about existing boundaries in new ways. Managers cling to the lines that separate one function from another or that divide customers from suppliers, in part because of cultural traditions and in part because of pressure for immediate results. If a redrawn boundary doesn't produce results now, it's not worth their time and effort.

Boundaries also provide the illusion of order in a world that is becoming increasingly chaotic. In complex, volatile times, people cling to the established order. Unconsciously, perhaps, they want to preserve traditional ways of relating. Partnering with a potential competitor, for instance, demands thinking about industry relationships in ways that feel threatening. Conducting business in developing countries requires adjustments that are confusing. Who wants to reframe boundaries and invite even more confusion and complexity into their lives?

Whole leaders do. They not only reframe the boundaries but they can emotionally accommodate the uncertainty of doing things in a new way; they can also take the risks of forming and maintaining "foreign" relationships.

Getting your head around the notion of moveable boundaries, though, is the first step, and what helps organizational leaders take it is awareness of the five different types of boundaries that they must reframe.

## Boundaries That Exist in
## Different Directions and Dimensions

Part of the challenge of boundary reframing is that a wide range of boundaries exists. As a result, a given executive may be capable of adapting to new geographical relationships but struggles with sharing information and resources with people in functions other than his own. By their very nature, boundaries are dividing lines and sometimes are crossed only at considerable peril. Boundaries are often psychological. Sometimes leaders make assumptions about the consequences of crossing boundaries, imagining problems that would never really materialize. Although it may be easier for a leader to cross one boundary without fear getting in his way, it may be more difficult to cross another one without feeling threatened.

Knowledge helps take some of the fear out of revising boundaries, so let's examine what each of the five types of boundaries— external, vertical, horizontal, geographical, and personal boundaries—entail.

### External Boundaries

External boundaries are defined by the invisible line between the organization and its environment. No longer can leaders maintain an insular mentality, only comparing the company's performance this year to its performance the previous year. It no longer matters if an individual is the best performer in the company or if one unit performs better than all other units. Everything now must be judged against world-class standards, which means looking at the world beyond the organization's borders.

This can create fear. It is much more reassuring to know that your inventory turns or that cycle times have increased 5 percent over the previous year than to learn that your performance is far below the best-in-class. Fear of acknowledging the gap between current performance and global standards keeps an insular focus. Thomas Friedman has made the point very clearly in *The World Is*

*Flat.* Because of technology, information flow, and lowered barriers to entry, the playing field of competition has been flattened and made smaller. Most professional work can now be done anywhere in the world around the clock, and so hungry would-be competitors in India, China, and Africa are now setting new standards for productivity and cost-efficiency.

Although companies collectively acknowledge that the world is flat, this awareness doesn't necessarily translate into an individual mind-set. As strange as it might seem, we have encountered many leaders who can acknowledge that competition is now literally coming from everywhere and that the only way to survive is to constantly challenge and increase performance, but who *consider this to be someone else's concern.* They don't translate this insight into implications for themselves.

## Vertical Boundaries

The manager–direct-report relationship used to have very clear boundaries, whether you were looking up or looking down. Today, not only are the terms *looking up* and *looking down* irrelevant, but the relationship between a direct report and her boss has changed and will continue to evolve. Managers must be both coach and mentor to others, and this means exhibiting greater transparency and emotional intelligence. As coaches and mentors, they must continuously empower their direct reports. In the other direction, managers are being held accountable by their bosses for providing highly detailed information (they are expected to know dashboards and metrics in depth), and this requirement is often confusing to managers who have empowered their own people and thus aren't as intimately involved in project details.

This boundary shift is especially hard for managers who are accustomed to telling people what to do and expecting them to do it. As one veteran manager remarked, "I didn't sign up to be Mr. Rogers." It is often difficult for results-focused managers to acknowledge their softer side, especially in the urgency of getting things done fast. To them, coaching, mentoring, and being transparent are stated values, but their behavior does not follow, usually because they place a higher value on reacting. In the back of their minds, they say to themselves, "I know this is important, but the immediate demands of my role take precedence." Providing their own leader with detailed knowledge also seems a distraction to the business of finding, selling, and keeping customers or clients. If they are not micromanaging, how are they supposed to know all the ins and outs of a project?

## Horizontal Boundaries

Since the Total Quality Management (TQM) movement in the 1980s, horizontal relationships have increased in importance. Understanding supply-chain management and delivering customer-integrated solutions demanded a level of partnership with customers and suppliers that was unprecedented in an earlier era. Even though more than twenty years have passed since TQM was introduced, and companies such as Wal-Mart, Federal Express, Dell, and many others have pioneered seamless integration with suppliers, a significant percentage of managers today still resist the idea of deep partnerships with vendors. Or they partner without enthusiasm, commitment, or true openness. Similarly, the growth of teams and "communities of interest" in organizations has made peer relationships more critical than ever before, but the idea of getting things done through peer influence rather than positional authority is not one every manager has embraced.

Though managers know they must manage these horizontal boundaries, they often don't do a very good job of it. Just as they were accustomed to thinking about boss-subordinate vertical relationships as one-up or one-down, they saw relationships with suppliers and colleagues as inherently unequal. The notion of partnering seemed unnatural. Although many of them have been forced to partner, they frequently do so in name only. People who resist reframing this boundary frequently are noncontributors on teams and unwilling to share information and ideas, or they fail to coach others to share.

## Geographical Boundaries

Here the boundary shifts are readily apparent. As companies become more decentralized, participate in joint ventures, create informal marketing or product development alliances, and engage in mergers and acquisitions throughout the world, old boundaries fall by the wayside. Working in unfamiliar cultures and being flexible when faced with different cultural approaches to business, leadership and negotiations can be challenging.

Some managers struggle with cross-cultural relationships beyond superficial conversation. They have difficulty adapting to the dominant cultural values of another country, wondering why business relationships can't be conducted on the same terms everywhere or, in other words, the way they're used to. Others attempt to force their approach on others, assuming that the American managerial way is the best way. In either case, these individuals don't accept that they must reframe these boundaries in a global, networked world.

## Personal Boundaries

In smaller organizations and simpler times, leaders were allowed their idiosyncrasies, even their dysfunctions. More than one highly esteemed CEO, even those who wrote books about their philosophy and success, were often tyrants or bullies in the name of performance. Today, people must manage their shadow side and personal weaknesses in order to live in a much more transparent, unforgiving, complex environment. The derailers that we discussed in *Why CEOs Fail*—aloofness, arrogance, volatility, for example—can undermine individual and organizational success if they are not acknowledged, understood, and managed. We cited the work of Bob Hogan in an earlier chapter. His research clearly points to the importance of personal traits in leaders' success. Qualities such as honesty and integrity, drive and ambition, openness to new ideas, energy and passion, and emotional intelligence have as much to do with successful leadership as intellect. Recognizing that personal traits are no longer off-limits and that who you are as a person affects how you perform as a manager and as a leader is crucial.

Some people adamantly refuse to acknowledge how their leadership personality creates the climate in which they lead others. They may be in denial about this effect, or they may believe that this type of self-analysis has no place in business. To be effective leaders, they must become continuously aware of how their vulnerabilities and shadow-side tendencies are diminishing their effectiveness and learn to manage them.

## Reframe, Don't Destroy

We want to emphasize that the cognitive imperative here is reframing and not eliminating boundaries. With all that has been written about boundaryless and matrixed organizations, it is easy to become confused. The holistic leader is not an anarchist who ignores boundaries as if they were the products of an evil system. Instead, holistic leaders embrace the paradox of boundaries. On the one hand, boundaries help people define purpose and focus. On the other hand, when they become too rigid and fixed in people's minds, they limit options for action. Ideally, people will learn to view them as permeable and shifting. In other words, they will become skilled at crossing existing boundaries when necessary and acknowledging when the vertical, horizontal, and other dividing lines have shifted.

In some matrix organizations, group decision making is required, and an effort is made to involve as many people as possible. Boundaries are ignored to facilitate sharing of divergent viewpoints and drive decision making to the right levels. Without these boundaries, though, chaos can be a consequence. In a matrixed company, you often have consultation without accountability; that is, everyone must be consulted before anything is done, but no one knows who is accountable. Boundaries provide accountability, as well as the structure and protocols necessary for operating efficiently.

Reframing these boundaries, therefore, feels dangerous. When the lines between manager and direct report, or company and vendor become blurred, and roles (and therefore accountability) are unclear, you glimpse the chaos of boundaryless organizations that we just described. The leader thinks, "How do I get my people to do what needs to be done if my positional power diminishes?" or "How can I trust my supplier with proprietary information?" or "How can I partner with a company in one area and compete with them in another?"

These are all legitimate questions, but reframing the boundaries doesn't mean ignoring the answers. It means respecting the boundaries but also being willing to transcend them when the situation warrants. At times, a boss must be very directive with his team. At other times, a boss needs to coach and influence his direct reports and allow them the freedom to achieve their goals through their own methods.

Another way to look at this paradox involves silos within organizations. Everyone from business gurus to the media has excoriated managers who remain mentally locked within their functional silos. Yet it remains incumbent on leaders to create a commitment to a given work unit or silo; the need remains for people to identify with their function and feel pride in what they do and camaraderie with those who share their area of expertise. At the same time, leaders must encourage their people to transcend these silos and become part of the wider enterprise. They must communicate that people should feel free to cross boundaries and contribute ideas and information to other functions if it helps achieve enterprise goals.

Tremendous benefits accrue to organizations when leaders can both observe and reframe boundaries. For instance, some leaders are able to keep their company's internal goals in mind but also see things through the eyes of the customer. As a result, they design systems and processes that make life easier for those within the company but also focus on customer needs. They are able to get past the old boundary dictating that a company should design the best processes for its own purposes; reframing the boundary allows them to factor in how those processes affect external stakeholders.

Similarly, leaders who can reframe horizontal boundaries are much better able to integrate supply chains into their organizations, thus reducing inventory costs and increasing delivery speed. This is a huge competitive advantage, but it requires people to accept that what the customer knows, the supplier knows. Some executives endorse the theory of partnering with suppliers, but when it comes to giving them immediate access via a shared Web site to sensitive information, they hesitate. As big as the benefit is, worst-case scenarios of suppliers communicating proprietary information to competitors causes them to reject the idea.

Perhaps the biggest benefit comes from reframing vertical boundaries. At a time when it is more critical than ever to develop talent from within rather than rely on recruiting it, managers must focus on their coaching and mentoring responsibilities. The more managers who reframe this boundary, the more talent an organization will attain. And it will attain talent faster. If, however, managers are unable to reconcile coaching and mentoring responsibilities with the pressure to deliver short-term results, this benefit will remain elusive.

## What Keeps Boundaries Fixed and Formidable

It is more than human nature that prevents otherwise smart, savvy people from reframing boundaries. While we are all resistant to change to a certain extent, boundary change comes with its own additional set of hurdles. Let's examine these hurdles and why they can be so difficult for some people to clear:

• *Incentive system hurdle.* Most organizational incentive systems reward behaviors that have proven successful in the past. Typically, meeting performance objectives is the standard measure, and it is relatively unusual to find incentive systems that encourage reframing the five boundaries (or even one of them). Part of the problem is that the ability to see boundaries in new ways is difficult to measure. More significantly, though, line leaders are often reluctant to reward behaviors that have not been proven to contribute to bottom-line success, such as the willingness and ability to develop leaders. In addition, even if leadership endorses boundary-reframing behaviors, a lag time exists between this endorsement and the restructuring of an incentive system.

• *Corporate culture hurdle*. As we've discussed previously, some cultures have norms and values that mitigate against boundary reframing. Successful companies, especially, have cultures that exert an enormous influence on behavior. If they have enjoyed unequal relationships with vendors for years, people find it difficult to break this pattern. Sometimes the influence of culture is not as overt as in the previous instance, operating instead at a subconscious level. A fiercely competitive culture, for instance, may have instilled such a strong win-lose attitude in people that they reflexively avoid forming any sort of alliance with companies that might compete with them in some arena. An executive in this type of company might not articulate his resistance as culturally based. He may simply reject this type of alliance as "not right for us." But beneath the surface his cultural indoctrination prevents him from reframing.

• *Arrogance hurdle*. This is akin to a country's xenophobia. Some organizations have such a superior attitude that they don't believe new relationships vertically, horizontally, or any which way will benefit them. Leaders don't feel it's worth their while to form an alliance with another company or deal with a personal derailer because they're already the best (at least in their own minds). They ask themselves, "What do we have to gain?" and answer, "Not enough." Enron is perhaps the recent example of an arrogant culture that could not deal with its own flaws and ignored the warning signs from the environment.

• *The "overwhelmed" hurdle*. Here the obstacle is feeling so stressed out that the leader lacks the time or energy to reframe boundaries. The mere thought of reframing feels exhausting. The leader is under so much pressure to perform that he is unwilling to do anything new or different that might detract from that performance.

As formidable as these obstacles are, they can be overcome through a variety of approaches. In our experience, three specific actions catalyze a boundary-reframing response.

## The Three Catalysts

If you want to help people adopt a reframing capability, you have a number of options, including the obvious strategy of restructuring the incentive system to reward boundary-reframing behaviors. We recognize, however, that not every organization can take such a "radical" step. Therefore, here are approaches that are easier to implement and that serve as catalysts to reframing:

• *Raise awareness that boundaries are changing.* It is surprising how many leaders don't read or look around outside their organizations or reflect on what they observe and either anticipate or consider how it will affect their companies. Perhaps that should not be surprising, given the hurdle of being overwhelmed. Nonetheless, awareness of shifting boundaries can be communicated in a number of ways. Leadership development programs can introduce new information and ideas about boundaries through presentations, as do visits to companies that are focusing on boundary issues, either through redesign, measurement, or leadership actions. Leaders can learn through seminars and workshops on related topics.

Ideally, growing awareness of the five boundary issues will cause people to form a theory of the case. Too often, they view problems caused by shifting boundaries as something to be managed or handled. With greater awareness, however, they start thinking about what might happen if they changed their approach to traditional boundaries—if they viewed alliances, joint ventures, and other partnerships with other functions or those outside as tools for growth rather than as tangential to enterprise goals. When people understand why something is happening, they are often better able to respond to it. We'll talk more in Chapter Six about how a theory of the case—a distinct point of view—can benefit organizations.

• *Take advantage when someone trips over a boundary.* People, especially successful people, are tremendously stubborn. Sometimes they need to run into a brick wall or find themselves failing because they didn't reframe a boundary before they become aware that they need to change. When people are on the edge of derailing, that's the time to intervene with coaching or leadership development. They need to get the message that if they don't change, they're dead. At this point, they may see it to their advantage to reframe boundaries.

• *Draw a distinction between organizational and individual arrogance.* Earlier, we noted that arrogance can be a hurdle to reframing. Certainly, some organizations foster this arrogance because they are so large and successful; they want to control the supply chain in ways that give them a significant competitive advantage. Organizations like Dell, Bank of America, and Wal-Mart set the rules, and their market superiority can filter down to the behavior of their leaders and managers. This is when people refuse to look at boundaries in fresh ways. They take the position that they are doing everything better than anyone else, so it makes no sense to consider new geographical or personal boundaries. What they don't realize, of course, is that their organization's superior position won't be maintained if they fail to reframe boundaries as circumstances dictate. Therefore, these top companies must make an extra effort to call attention to individual arrogance and discourage it. They must provide feedback that points out to people where their arrogance is causing them to be inflexible regarding internal and external relationships. They should also distinguish between taking pride in accomplishments and lording those accomplishments over others.

We do not underestimate the power of boundaries. As any observer of world affairs knows, countries consider their boundaries inviolate and go to war when another country reframes them. It behooves leaders to be flexible about boundaries at certain times and under certain circumstances. However, seeing boundaries from a new vantage point can lead to the establishment of potentially beneficial relationships that never existed in the past.

◆ ◆ ◆

As we'll see in the next chapter, reframing boundaries and practicing the other cognitive behaviors we've discussed set the stage for the next cognitive skill: execution—or getting things done.

# 5

# GETTING THINGS DONE

In recent years, there has been a great deal of talk around the topic of getting things done. Larry Bossidy and Ram Charan's best-selling book, *Execution*, has certainly catalyzed the discussion about leaders who are great thinkers but not-so-great doers. Despite all this talk, however, we have found that much confusion still exists around this capability. Sometimes, leaders oversimplify the topic and view execution as a matter of cracking the whip and driving people hard. In other instances, leaders take the opposite position and attempt to use influence to get others to execute effectively.

Like most leadership skills, however, execution is more complicated than either of these approaches suggest. To get things done, leaders need to grasp the complexity of the task and find an approach that takes the difficulties associated with execution into consideration. Head, heart, and guts leaders are able to do this, in part, because they recognize that people issues and risk can affect what is accomplished.

Perhaps the best way to start our examination of this cognitive strength is by examining two common leadership types and how these types (strategic or operational) approach execution.

## Strategic or Operational, Rarely Both

Some leaders are pure strategists, brilliant analyzers of data, and setters of direction. They may even be visionaries, able to transcend the conventional thinking and create something new and different for their organizations. They may be adept at inspiring and moti-vating people to believe in their strategies, but they aren't particu-larly good at figuring out how to implement them. They often are bored with the details of putting things into practice and leave that to others. Some may even believe that if the strategy is right, it should almost execute itself.

Some leaders are operations-driven. They love getting their hands dirty. They thrive on finding solutions to difficult problems, and they relish the details. They are always thinking about how to get from Point A to Point B as quickly and cost-effectively as possi-ble. Pragmatic and focused, they are not usually "big idea" people. To get things done, they work hard and get others to work hard. They usually fail to consider how an idea can capture people's imag-inations and inspire them to work harder and more creatively than ever before. When it comes to a choice between an innovative-but-moderately-risky approach versus a standard-but-less-risky tack, they will choose the latter every time.

From around 1980 to 2000, there was a strong view in the busi-ness press, encouraged by business school executive programs, that leaders should be strategic and that operations was a function rather than a set of leadership activities. It was enough for leaders to cre-ate solid strategies. In fact, the conventional wisdom was that it was better if strong leaders stayed away from the executional details—that they would just get in the way of the people who knew what they were doing. The focus was on visionary leadership, and many CEOs of the period were celebrated for their strategic vision.

Bossidy and Charan's book helped change this prevailing notion, insisting that leaders must be on top of operational details if they wanted to execute successfully. A framework for execution has emerged that is far more performance-oriented and demanding of leaders than in the past. It is no longer enough to have the right people in the room when formulating a strategy, according to Cha-ran. You have to have the right conversations with the right peo-ple, they have to be in the right jobs, and you need the right follow-up mechanisms in place to make sure they are doing their jobs effectively.

This is not an operational mind-set. Although the operational details are important, they can become too important and hamper execution. We know of more than one executive who gives his team their goals and then gives them the methods to reach those goals. The key is being aware of the details but not using them to disempower your organization.

Admittedly, this can be a difficult proposition. If you're the head of a business, and you see a key business unit or high-performer begin to decline, do you intervene, take charge, and violate the chain of command? Or do you stand back and hope that things will right themselves? People tend to answer these questions by either taking extreme positions or moving back and forth between them. They are always into the details (operational extreme) or refuse to have anything to do with them (strategic extreme).

A much more effective approach, however, is finding the balance between the two positions. The ability to know when to be operational and when to be strategic is crucial. Getting things done often means knowing when to get them done by taking charge and being directive and when to step back, trust others, and provide direction. It also means moving back and forth between these two positions with alacrity.

Ken Lewis, chairman and CEO of Bank of America, has mastered the balance between operations and strategy, and he is brilliant at getting things done. He took a vision-driven organization run by a dealmaker and turned it into a Six Sigma–focused company where people deliver what they promise and know precisely what is expected of them. By giving people at all levels specific tools and metrics that are derived from Six Sigma methodology, Lewis has enforced fact-based decision making. Leaders at all levels of Bank of America now honor their commitments to each other, engage in disciplined meetings, focus on fact-based decisions, and measure progress against stated objectives. The change in the culture of the bank is remarkable and is reflected in the market value of the company. In addition, Ken has turned over more than half the senior ranks, replaced them with the right people, no matter what predecessor bank they worked in, and instituted a highly competitive, growth-oriented, execution-driven culture. As he continues to buy new banks, there is little difficulty integrating them successfully and fulfilling the promises made to the Street, evidenced most recently by the acquisitions of Fleet Bank and MBNA.

Lest you think Lewis was only an operational guy, he has deftly shifted the organization's strategy recently so that it focuses on organic growth. His earlier operational approach helped the company reach its goal as the most admired company in financial services, but his next goal was to make Bank of America one of the *world's* most admired companies, and for that, he needed to shift his strategic perspective from execution to how to grow the bank's revenue without relying entirely on acquisitions. As a result, he has focused on developing leaders, working across boundaries, and creating a "Universal Bank" model and mind-set as ways to achieve organic growth.

In addition, Lewis's style as a leader reflects this shift. Rather than the detail-focused, operational leader of the past, by his own admission he has become less hands-on, more reflective, and more focused on longer-term strategy, allowing the great performers he has surrounded himself with to deliver the results.

In the future, Lewis may move back to his earlier operational style, which is fine if it fits the situation. The point, though, is that his ability to move between operational and strategic approaches enhances his ability to get things done.

## What Stands in the Way of a Lewis-Like Mind-Set

Developing the capacity to think both operationally and strategically and accomplish ambitious goals would be easier to do if it were not for four factors that affect every leader. Let's examine these factors (functional bias, need for control, the imposition of style and preferences, and process overload) and learn why they prevent people from executing as well as they otherwise might.

## Functional Bias

Function predisposes people to be operational or strategic, based on early developmental experiences. If you came up through marketing, you're encouraged to examine customer trends and patterns, and you tend to take a wider and longer view rather than a detail-oriented one, making you more of a strategic thinker. If you came up through finance and have managed complex financial issues, you're likely to be more operational because a background in accounting or measurement creates this foundation. The marketing person tends to look at the world through the lens of his functional experience, analyzing situations and coming up with ideas to deal with problems; he is unlikely to dictate moves to his people or "get his hands dirty," since he has become accustomed to having an impact by thinking conceptually and strategically. The finance person typically focuses on the measurements, since even a small error in the financial area can lead to greater errors in calculation and reporting. And in the current economic and regulatory climate, there is great pressure to get the numbers right and hit short-term financial targets. Consequently, she may not make mistakes but may need to be encouraged to take a step back and solve problems through innovative thinking.

Functional bias also stands in the way of people getting things done through others. Technology is a driver of teamwork and productivity today. If you are not technologically literate beyond the use of e-mail and the Internet, you need to increasingly rely on those with this expertise. In fact, cross-functional collaboration has become so important that if you maintain a silo mentality, you'll have difficulty accomplishing much outside your narrow range of expertise. Whether you're coming from a strategic or operational bias, you need to create trusting lateral relationships, not only with people in other functions but with vendors, customers, and competitors. Leaders who are so functionally narrow that they can't establish these relationships struggle as soon as they are placed in situations that demand real collaboration.

## Need for Control

Despite the overall movement toward a knowledge-based economy, the Industrial Age management practices do not die easily. In an unpredictable, complex, and interdependent world of intangible outputs, the leadership default reflex is to exert control. This reflex, though, can have the opposite effect. At the extreme, "control freaks" rob others of initiative and creativity; their micromanaging style fosters a sense of cynicism and risk-aversion. Though being overcontrolling is more likely to occur in an operational mind-set than a strategic one, it can have an impact on both types of leaders. Strategic types can obsess over every nuance of their strategy, moving at a snail's pace as they attempt to gather more and more information to support every aspect of the strategy. As good as their vision might be, it is implemented too slowly or is too laden with research and study to create impact. Operational types who focus on control create disengagement. Volatile operational leaders lose their temper at even inconsequential mistakes or are so wrapped up in the details that they lose sight of their larger purpose. For example, they may expend a lot of their energy on implementing a new orientation process by a given deadline but fail to think through the best way to communicate the policy throughout the company so people understand and support it.

We're not suggesting that forsaking control is a key to execution. Obviously, you need to exert control to keep yourself informed of details and have metrics in place to measure progress. When control becomes the goal rather than the means to a larger end, however, execution is hampered.

We know one brilliant leader who is obsessed with the details of his organization. He enjoys running meetings with thorough agendas, prides himself on mastering the details of everyone's operations, and knows the budget inside and out. He is a tinkerer, and he believes that if the "machine is well tuned" the organization will produce. What he misses, however, is the human energy that real motivation creates. His attempts to measure output stifle creativity, and he is unable to unlock the passion and commitment that drives real execution.

## Imposition of Style and Preferences

This is as opposed to adapting your own style and preferences to the job. Historically, the former philosophy (the imposition of style) has been how leaders in business have approached their role. An individual who was inherently stubborn displayed this obstinacy as a manager and as a leader, and most of the time it wasn't a major roadblock to getting things done. In fact, it helped her achieve certain objectives.

Today, this same stubbornness can be a major roadblock. In an interdependent environment, leaders need to recognize when their style and preferences are hampering execution. They don't have to do a 180-degree personality change, but they do need to be alert for situations where their dominant style is ineffective. By being aware that their single-mindedness is preventing an important matter from being resolved, they can step back and ask themselves if this trait is more a minus than a plus in a particular situation. It may help them back off and work harder to resolve a stalemate.

Every leader has a style, but too often he refuses to change it because it has been indirectly reinforced through previous success or he is unaware of its impact. Flexibility and awareness are crucial today for implementing effective solutions. Many companies invest significantly in helping their leaders understand their preferred style through preference testing such as the Myers-Briggs Typology Inventory or the FIRO-B or many other tools. These assessments can help leaders understand that their preferred style of leading may not work in every situation, and without flexibility and a broad repertoire, any preferred way of operating can be a major deficiency without awareness and adaptation.

Finally, leaders are often unaware that different circumstances require different types of styles. The same type of directive approach that may be necessary in a crisis involving a turnaround would be completely ineffective if the challenge is to empower an organization to generate ideas that can drive growth. Similarly, operating in a staff role in which little authority is vested in a position is radically different from having line responsibility and ultimate accountability for financial performance. The former places great emphasis on the ability to influence and requires a completely different approach to leadership. We have known exceptional leaders who struggle when they find themselves in a situation that requires them to change their style of operating.

## Too Many Processes

Understandably, CEOs and other leaders often want to put in a new process or system in order to increase or improve measurement and performance. A technological development may lead to a new manufacturing process, improved access to a customer database, or financial accounting methods. On the surface, investment in new software and processes helps get things done with greater speed and quality. Be aware, however, that too many processes can overwhelm an organization and detract from, rather than enhance, execution. Organizations suffering from process overload become internally focused. They direct so much of their attention to processes and metrics that they may ignore the underlying behavior that creates success. For example, they may lose their external focus and pay less attention to the clients and opportunities; they may focus all their attention on making the new processes work.

How many processes are too many? We can't give you a number, but we witness many companies today that are suffering from process overload. If you can't identify the number of processes in which you are an active participant, then the odds are that you're inviting process overload. A diagnosis of the organization and an attitude survey will tell you whether people are overwhelmed by the interdependencies and communication requirements of all the new systems the company has put in place. If they are overwhelmed, they are not going to be able to get things done as effectively as they might, since they have taken their eye off some of the external stakeholders for whom they're trying to get things done. We see many corporate attitude surveys today, and work complexity due to process overload is a common complaint.

## Getting Things Done in a Chaotic, Unforgiving Environment

If you can overcome the four obstacles just described, you still face environmental challenges to executing effectively. Timeframes are shorter, standards are higher, pressure to exceed the previous quarter's results is greater, and comparative data are always there. With a smaller margin for error and a greater need to take smart risks, leaders cannot execute using the playbook from the previous year, or even quarter. The first thing leaders must do, therefore, is to follow our earlier recommendation to find a balance between strategic and operations mind-sets. If you don't understand your dominant mind-set, solicit feedback from your direct reports; they are usually very much aware of your preferred mode. Finding a balance in your style will create situational options when the dominant way of executing doesn't work. In a rapid, overworked, constantly communicating environment, assume that your dominant approach won't work in many situations, and you may even be a prisoner of your own experience.

The second tactic that we've alluded to involves developing influence through lateral relationships to get things done. This may seem counterintuitive to traditional leaders who are accustomed to executing vertically, but the ability to include others and to influence without direct authority is becoming the key ingredient to success in complex environments. Working within cross-functional teams, creating win-win partnerships with suppliers, forming alliances with companies in related industries or fields, and even entering into joint ventures with competitors can create productive outputs without needing to own or control resources.

Third, create a climate of accountability. When people contribute because they feel they have to—that the company is forcing them to produce—they lack the commitment and creativity necessary to execute effectively. One leader we know refers to this as "malicious compliance"! Establishing accountability means creating performance consequences that are fair. This also means that leaders model keeping commitments and accepting consequences. They establish this sense of commitment and responsibility in people. A child psychology concept is useful here: the notion of the "autotelic" child. Many children do well in school because of extrinsic motivation, such as their wish to please parents or teachers, or in response to threats from parents. *Autotelic* means their motivation is intrinsic, that they achieve because of something inside them. Developing that same internal motivation in organizations is what accountability is all about. An autotelic workforce has a high capacity for getting things done.

The fourth recommendation is this: value and display perseverance. There is no substitute for stick-to-it-iveness. Leaders can become easily distracted and reactive in business today, when they are bombarded with stimuli, communication, requests, information, and choices. You probably know more than one leader who starts projects but never finishes them. Perseverance is a guts trait used in the service of the cognitive. If you want to get things done, you need to display the courage of your convictions. No doubt, leaders are tempted to back off when their pet project develops a glitch or when a program falls out of political favor. If they truly believe in it, though, it behooves them to stick with it. Not only will this help them accomplish a goal they perceive as worthwhile, but it sends a message to their people that perseverance is a quality they value. In many studies of innovative products and breakthrough ideas in companies, there is clear evidence of a "Lazarus effect"—referring to an idea champion who refused to let a new approach or product idea die and created eventual success from a dismal beginning and early resistance.

Fifth, leverage people's strengths rather than help them fix their weaknesses. This is a heart trait in service of execution. Too many leadership development programs are all about fixing people. No doubt, some leaders need fixing. The problem is one of attitude. When leaders adopt the perspective that something is wrong with others, they disempower them, even as they are trying to help them. We have found that most individuals are willing to sacrifice for a system that cares about them, that considers them assets worth developing. They are not willing to sacrifice for a system that sees them as flawed and weak. Tough-as-nails executives talk a lot about "executing the hell out of a project" but say their people don't care. Fear and tough talk will only get people to do so much. Leveraging direct reports' strengths means collaborating with them—capitalizing and building on what they're good at to achieve a common goal. It's important to surface and address behaviors that need to be modified or changed, but that should not be the primary focus of development.

Sander Flaum, now a consultant to the pharmaceutical and biotech industries, understood how to get things done. Though this story takes place several years ago, it is an important example because it captures certain traits we've just discussed, especially perseverance and leveraging people's strengths to accomplish goals.

When Flaum became CEO of Robert A. Becker, a healthcare advertising agency, it was in serious trouble, about to lose two of the agency's biggest clients. Shortly thereafter, the agency essentially had only one major client—Bristol-Myers—and that account was shaky. At first, no one would even return Flaum's phone calls. Everyone told him he had made a mistake joining Becker and that he should get out before it was too late.

Flaum, though, was a whole leader who knew how to get things done. He began by creating what he referred to as "a culture of persistence." He instilled in his people the notion that some day they would be working for clients with the biggest products in the pharmaceutical business. He emphasized the need to be relentless, even in the face of initial rejection, and demonstrated this relentlessness when Bristol-Myers did not ask them to be in on the pitch for Buspar—an anti-anxiety drug. Rather than accept this rejection, Flaum and his team lobbied the Bristol-Myers product director with idea after idea for the project, and they were eventually asked to make a pitch. They won the business, and their resulting campaign for Buspar created a dramatic increase in sales.

It also seems clear that Flaum was astute about leveraging his people's strengths as idea creators. This is an ad agency's stock in trade, but Flaum saw that he could get more and better ideas out of his people if he encouraged them to apply their creativity at every opportunity. As Flaum has written, "Never call a client without a big idea." That became the agency's mantra. As a result, Becker developed a reputation for superior creativity and attracted clients that at the agency's low points seemed to never even return phone calls. Eventually, Becker was named ad agency of the year and had seven of the ten top pharmaceutical companies as clients.

Interestingly, Flaum wrote in a *Pharmaceutical Times* article that "we did it with our brains and our hearts, but most of all, we did with sweat." We would translate *sweat* to mean that Flaum had the courage of his convictions, and he was willing to work with incredible persistence to accomplish his goals.

## Banishing the Old Model of a Leader Who Executes

Despite all we have learned about how to get things done, organizations still gravitate toward leaders who are "tough" (that is, controlling and directive) when they are desperate for improved performance. They want someone who is not afraid to take action, keep moving forward, and not display weakness. *Action* usually means to cut budgets and staff, initiate yet another strategy, and drive people toward an outcome. We would remind these organizations to consider the fate of Sunbeam Corporation when they brought in "Chainsaw" Al Dunlap—a noted tough-guy and cost-cutter. He lasted less than two years, managing to fire half the workforce and make a bad situation worse; Sunbeam went into bankruptcy a few years after Dunlap was fired.

Although getting things done and increasing performance may mean cutting people and costs, this should not be a knee-jerk reaction. Heart and guts enter into the equation, and ruthless martinets or anxious CEOs display little guts and less heart. Organizations should use Ken Lewis, Bill Weldon, and Andrea Jung as models of leaders who execute well—whole leaders who get things done, not only because they are smart about how to do it but because they inspire people to work harder and better and because they display the courage that staying the course demands.

It is possible to develop leaders who execute but only if the development process substitutes a new model for the old one. Perhaps it's counterintuitive, but you don't get things done by relying on force and fear. Development should present exemplars from within the company by way of demonstrating this point; it should give participants the opportunity to understand internal business units or visit external companies that execute well because leaders blend head, heart, and guts to create a culture where people want to get things done. And it should offer each leader the chance to revise his own theory of the case about how to execute. This last point can be a challenging one, and it may require real-world experiences (such as the ones in Action Learning programs), in which people are given an ambitious task that can only be accomplished by using the three qualities of a whole leader. People—especially hard-headed people—must learn that some situations require risk and empathy rather than just a strong plan communicated in a forceful manner. It sometimes takes a public failure—an instance where all the shouting and hard-nosed decisions don't get something done—before an individual is willing to rethink his method.

When that happens, though, a leader is much more likely to try other approaches to accomplish his goals.

◆ ◆ ◆

In the next chapter, we complete our formal coverage of the cognitive side of leadership—what we are calling head leadership—by describing how the development of a point of view can be valuable to a company.

# 6

# DEVELOPING AND ARTICULATING A POINT OF VIEW

This last trait in our cognitive section may seem less of a priority than the others, but in reality it is every bit as critical. At first glance, developing a point of view may appear to be a luxury rather than a necessity. After all, compared to cognitive abilities such as getting things done and reframing boundaries, developing a point of view doesn't sound as timely or as useful. A point of view, however, serves as an anchor and a driver. At a time when many leaders feel uncertain and uncommitted, a point of view offers an internal sense of security—a base from which decisions can be made in a sometimes political, complex, and unclear corporate environment. A point of view also helps leaders maintain a consistent, credible persona; it can generate the commitment and passion necessary to achieve ambitious goals, and it can help them stay motivated and involved, providing a sense of purpose as they move forward in their careers.

Unfortunately, we have observed many leaders who, instead of formulating a point of view, simply take on the most politically correct or astute perspective. This is an era when leaders, in the name of getting ahead, cynically or pessimistically take stances they don't believe in. No doubt, you are aware of senior executives who have been willing to change positions, depending on what their boss or board expects, or have adopted positions that they have reservations about. As smart and talented as some leaders are, they are vulnerable to "pointless views," especially when they seem prudent from a career perspective.

What these leaders don't realize is that without a point of view, they rarely inspire others and get them to sign on with them. They may fool themselves into thinking that "fitting in" will help their careers, but in the long term, it will prevent them from being seen as effective leaders.

## Why People Fail to Develop Their Beliefs and Take a Stand

Here is an illustration of what we mean:

> Carole was a top executive at a major corporation. Smart, savvy, and highly successful at a relatively young age, Carole was scheduled to make a major presentation to the executive committee of her company. She worked hard on the presentation, which revolved around her function's strategy and how it dovetailed with larger business goals. Her presentation went well, or so Carole thought. She was smooth and articulate; her PowerPoint was crisp; she didn't go on too long or skip over any key points, and she knew that what she had to say was consistent with the CEO's philosophy and approach. Carole had great respect for the CEO, who was considered by many to be one of the top leaders in the country and who had focused on a few clear priorities that had helped turn the company around. She wanted to be sure he saw her as "on the team" and that her presentation meshed with his ideas for the organization's direction.

In fact, Carole's presentation alienated everyone in the room. They viewed her talk as simply being propaganda for the CEO's positions. If they had closed their eyes and changed the voice they were hearing from female to male, they could have been listening to the CEO. It quickly became clear that Carole had not developed her own point of view; she borrowed one. If Carole had presented her own ideas and arguments and *then* demonstrated how they linked to other business priorities, including those of the CEO, she would have been effective. Her presentation, however, came off as politically motivated and self-centered, and in this important snap-shot, Carole lost credibility with the executive committee.

You would think that someone as smart as Carole would have recognized that loyalty is not always leadership. You would assume that her intelligence and her experiences would automatically pro-duce a distinct point of view. Carole, though, fell victim to forces larger than herself.

Let us look at the forces that cause people to avoid developing or acting on a point of view:

• *The mistaken notion that leaders should represent the organiza-tional party line.* People confuse loyalty to the organization with fur-thering its goals. The latter can be achieved through critical challenge and questioning, not blindly embracing everything the company stands for and endorsing all the current strategies and tac-tics. Certainly, it behooves every leader to work for an organization in which he believes, and if a given individual disagrees with every-thing, it is probably best that he leave. Many leaders, however, sub-scribe so fully and so mindlessly to the organizational point of view that they don't have the space to develop their own. They may have convinced themselves along the way that this mind-set is best for the company and represents their loyalty to it. They may be so anxious about how they are evaluated by their boss or superiors that they are literally afraid to disagree in any meaningful way. Most likely, though, they haven't taken the time to think about the enterprise beyond their cubicle or office; they leave the thinking to others because there is so much else to get done.

• *Organizational environments that encourage strict adherence to the party line.* Though these types of companies are less overt, fast-moving cultures in competitive environments demand that people be "on the bus." We often ask leaders to identify the unwritten rules of an organization. Frequently, the number-one written rule is this: "Do not express disagreement with your boss." This rule is sometimes more operative the higher you go in a company in which a strong culture discourages dissent among those at the top.

Sometimes "alignment" becomes more important than good decision making, and leaders with a strong point of view are seen as contentious and distracting. Implicitly, some corporations don't want people to express disagreement about strategies and policies; they prefer consensus on all issues. They want adherence to the cultural values until something goes wrong, and then the prevailing view becomes, "Why didn't more people speak up?" In these companies, people may well develop a point of view, but they dare not express it. Or they save it for the Internet chat board, which is usually alive with insights, information, and ideas.

• *A failure to read, investigate, and think about what's happening in the "outside" world.* To form a point of view, you need to create friction with a diversity of external sources. This means reading about best practices, high-performing companies, excellent leaders, and so on. It also means participating in conferences, meeting other leaders, and understanding the forces that surround the world in which you live, such as macroeconomics, politics, environmental issues, geopolitical forces, and demographics. And, finally, it means reflection—stepping back and mulling over everything you have read and experienced in order to formulate your perspective. It is difficult to form a point of view in an experiential and knowledge vacuum; you need to integrate information and ideas from diverse sources.

When we begin coaching a senior leader, one of the first questions we ask is, "What do you read?" From this question, we can gain insight into how a leader develops her point of view from divergent and differing sources. You need to rub your ideas against those of others in order to generate some heat and light. From this mental energy, you'll develop a theory about what is important to you as a leader and how business should be conducted.

• *Self-doubt about one's ability to form a point of view.* Leaders may be confident in other areas—in their areas of functional expertise, for instance—but they don't see themselves as great thinkers with strong opinions about leadership topics. Developing a point of view isn't just the job of academicians or senior-level people, Unfortunately, for many leaders, critical thinking and analysis stops when business school ends. Everyone naturally has her own theory of how work gets done in a company, the type of leadership that inspires others to follow, and why a given strategy is so effective. Many times, though, these theories are subconscious, and people don't have sufficient faith in their own experiences and thinking processes to bring them to the surface. Instead, they leave it to others to form a point of view, and they just do the work.

Many leaders enjoy and learn from leadership programs that develop leaders rather than train them. In developmental programs, great teachers encourage leaders to think, challenge, reflect, discuss, and debate. It can be exciting work, and for many leaders it is the first time in a long time they've engaged in real critical thinking. And they like it.

## What "Point of View" Means

The definition of the term *point of view* may seem self-evident, but it can be tricky to define in practical terms. It is something broader than one view of one subject (for example, a belief that global experience is necessary for leadership). It is also more specific than a particular belief (for example, in the movie *Wall Street,* the main character, Gordon Gecko, summarizes his business philosophy by saying, "Greed is good"). A viewpoint is an overarching, strongly held system of beliefs that apply to everything from individual behavior to values to business strategy. A leader can use his point of view to evaluate a specific option or opportunity—for example, to determine whether he believes a new growth strategy will be effective, to assess whether a corporate practice is unethical, and to evaluate which of his direct reports deserves a promotion. A point of view, in other words, provides a framework for analysis and decision making.

Two of the leaders we have referred to in this book—Ken Lewis of Bank of America and Andrea Jung of Avon—have powerful points of view. Ken is driven by his belief that Bank of America can be the best financial institution and most admired company in the world, and his strategic choices flow from this conviction. Andrea believes in direct sales and the power of the brand, and she has not wavered in this belief, using it to convince skeptics, reinvigorate a company many people had given up on, and recruit top people to her cause.

Bill George, David's former boss at Honeywell and later the CEO of Medtronic, developed and articulated a point of view. His notion of "authentic leadership" (he also wrote a book about this subject) consists of forming meaningful connections with people, motivating with mission, displaying caring, and acting on values. As a leader, he emphasized being "real" and wearing your values on your sleeve. As a result, he was not shy about communicating his authenticity, even if it didn't fit with the conventional wisdom. At one point, he said, "Shareholders come third"—a quote that was widely reported in the media. Bill believes that companies should put their customers first and empower their employees to meet customer needs, and if this is done, they will achieve better returns for shareholders than companies that focus on Wall Street more than any other group. Given Medtronic's growth and profits during George's twelve-year tenure—its market capitalization went from $1.1 billion to $460 billion—it's clear that his distinctive point of view paid dividends.

We don't want to oversimplify this concept. Bill George's point of view, for instance, didn't suddenly appear in a moment of epiphany. It took a long time to form, and Bill adjusted aspects of it based on changes in the environment. Although authentic leadership was his focus, he applied it in different ways in different situations. This last point is crucial. Points of view are not set in stone. They are strongly held, certainly, but they are not dogmatic or unyielding. Paradox management theory provides insight into how to "hold" a point of view effectively and has been described effectively in the book *Polarity Management* by Barry Johnson.

To manage a paradox, you must appreciate the argument that is diametrically opposed to your own, and you must communicate your appreciation. When you acknowledge an opposing viewpoint, you make your own position more acceptable. A paradox will seem impossible to manage if you take a black-or-white stance. It becomes manageable when you have the mental flexibility to hold two seemingly opposing concepts in your head. You make your viewpoint palatable to others when you acknowledge their opposing perspective and demonstrate that you understand it and empathize with it.

In paradox management, you don't compromise. In the same way, the leader with a strong perspective doesn't say something like, "Well, now that you've explained your ideas, I'll incorporate some of them." This would only diminish a point of view. Instead, this leader acknowledges, "I have this point of view now, but at some future point, it may be that your point of view is valid. Right now, though, this is how I see things."

As is the case with our other cognitive traits, this one also requires heart and guts. Developing a point of view usually starts as a thought process—the integration of diverse experiences and concepts into a larger perspective. People with viewpoints, however, don't always express them. Noel Tichy emphasizes the importance of having a "teachable" point of view, and this incorporates into the heart area. What is your capacity to persuade others to your way of viewing the world? Are you able to connect with others through your point of view? Do the people around you know what your point of view is? Does your way of seeing things energize those around you and secure commitments toward achieving a goal?

Then there is the issue of what you *do* with your point of view? Acting on it requires courage. You may have to take significant financial risks to adhere to your point of view; you may have to take the chance of offending powerful people in your company or alienating clients because of decisions that you feel are essential.

> Ron—a senior vice president with a large company—knew of a plan under consideration to eliminate 10 percent of the headcount in his company. It wasn't the downsizing itself that ran counter to Ron's

point of view. Instead, it was the plan's insistence that the head-count reduction be carried out in the most economical manner pos-sible—that is, more expensive people (in terms of salary and benefits) should be eliminated over less expensive ones.

Ron strongly believed in the notion of being human first and a leader second. All his work life he had found that productivity always was higher long term when groups were led by humanistic leaders rather than bureaucrats or self-aggrandizing showmen. He was certain the economical downsizing was not only wrong ethically but would hurt relationships with a portion of the 90 percent who remained. At a meeting to finalize the headcount reduction plan, Ron spoke out against this aspect of the plan and suggested an alter-native. Though Ron made some enemies because of his interven-tion, he remained with the company and is now one of three possible successors to the outgoing CEO.

With this story in mind, we should emphasize that organiza-tions would not run particularly efficiently if the ten top leaders pos-sessed ten radically different points of view. Fortunately, this is not usually the case. Most leaders in an organization who have been there for a sustained period of time tend to share at least some com-mon ground. In effective executive teams, they may see things dif-ferently at times, but they have learned how to use those differences productively, challenging each other without acrimony or hidden agendas. It is one of the most difficult challenges of being a senior executive today: how to balance the strong opinions and leadership required of an individual leader with the need to listen, incorporate, and integrate as a member of a senior team.

Effective executive teams acknowledge the CEO's point of view and respond to it, giving it appropriate deference in the end but maintaining an independent point of view in the process of devel-oping a decision. At Mercer Delta, consultants use the "wave the-ory of communications" to explain how ideas and strategies cascade down through an organization: the CEO puts forth his ideas for the future of the company; the next level takes the CEO's viewpoint and reinterprets it for the next level down; that level, in turn, reinterprets it for the people below them. Ideally, the message that cascades down is not exactly the same as the one the CEO delivered. Instead, reinterpretation allows someone at each level to inject his point of view and explain the message's relevance, not only to the company but to the next level down. The original message remains constant, but reinterpretation allows it to become relevant for different groups.

Reinterpretation of organizational messages, therefore, is how leaders inject their point of view into the mix.

## The Five-Step Process

Corporations can do a lot to help people develop their point of view, and to facilitate that development, they should be aware of the typical process by which an individual develops a point of view and uses it productively.

### Step 1: Define the Challenge

People begin to formulate or revise their point of view when something in their environment prompts them to clarify how they see things. Perhaps you are called upon to come up with new ideas for revenue growth, and the prospect of challenging the current business model or developing a new approach to selling, marketing, or prospecting catalyzes your need to assess a point of view. A cognitive challenge or one involving risk, too, can prompt you to step back and ask yourself hard questions about how a specific event fits your theory of the case. Whatever the challenge is, it jars you out of your usual mind-set and demands that you fit it into a larger, personal perspective.

### Step 2: Explore External Information

The second step is to explore external information sources related to the challenge. In other words, read and absorb information. When you start forming your point of view, you must filter it through outside (that is, outside yourself) sources of information and ideas. Books, articles, and Web sites help shape a perspective in an informed manner. Many executives develop the bad habit of reading only material, especially periodicals and newspapers, they consistently agree with. Force yourself to wander around in the deluge of information available today to challenge your own biases and assumptions.

## Step 3: Converge Ideas into a Single Viewpoint

After absorbing a diverse group of ideas, the next step is to ask yourself, "What do I believe?" and "Why do I believe it's true?" This step causes you to integrate what is useful and helps you focus your point of view and have a clear and concise way of seeing an issue through your own values and perspective.

## Step 4: Test the Idea with Others

Engage in dialogue and debates with other people about how you see the business. Allow others whom you respect, especially including direct reports, to hear and challenge your philosophy about the enterprise, direction, competition, values, and strategy. How do they respond? Are they inspired and in complete agreement with what you suggest? Do they debate you on certain points? The important point is to have a real conversation and practice articulating what you believe. In many leadership development programs we run, we devote a whole session to "Stand and Deliver," in which executives practice formulating, articulating, and presenting their point of view on the business and then obtain the feedback of their peers.

## Step 5: Reconfigure Your Viewpoint

Reconfigure your viewpoint *and then take some risks with it*. Based on feedback and dialogue, you may need to modify your perspective. Once you've modified it, you're ready to put it to use. Let it guide your positions on some key business issues. Obviously, you must use judgment as to when and on what issues to take this risk, but this is where both you and the organization stand to benefit the most. Every company needs leaders who act on the basis of strongly held beliefs, and this is your chance to be such a leader. Finally, make sure that you challenge yourself to make your point of view current. Don't let it become dogma. Be open to modifications in light of changing circumstances and your own evolving view of the world around you.

Companies should do everything possible to allow their leaders to take these five steps. This can mean everything from creating an environment conducive to developing a point of view (especially Step 5) to providing coaching and workshops to facilitate taking these five steps.

For instance, when coaching senior executives with this goal in mind, we ask some of the following questions:

- What is happening in the world in terms of economic, technological, or business-specific trends?
- What are you paying particular attention to and why?
- What does it mean to you, your group, and your company?

We also ask them to place themselves in the following situation:

> Imagine I have gathered together ten people in the company who know you better than anyone else here. If I ask them what you stand for as a leader, what might they say? Would they be able to articulate it? Would they each have a different opinion? What they be persuaded by your point of view? Would they be inspired by it and your enthusiasm for and commitment to it?

In addition, we coach people to incorporate storytelling into how they express their point of view. Too often, leaders express their perspectives through facts and figures or through a dry articulation of their ideas. To be effective, a point of view should be expressed compellingly. People respond strongly to perspectives delivered with passion and purpose, and stories are tools to evoke this response. Roger Schank, author of *Virtual Learning*, is one of the world's top authorities on how people learn, and he believes that stories are a far more effective teaching tool than lecturing. Their emotional component, combined with the drama inherent in a story, makes the lesson more memorable.

Dan Vasella, chairman of Novartis, communicates his point of view powerfully through storytelling. Central to the Novartis strategy is developing successful drugs to combat cancer, and while he makes a compelling business case for this focus, he also is adept at sharing his viewpoint, both as a physician and as someone who has lost his sister to cancer. The stories he tells are moving and powerful, and they demonstrate his conviction that this is the right direction for Novartis but a meaningful and contributing role for everyone in the company. No one doubts for a second that this is a CEO who believes in what he is doing, and after listening to him, everyone wants to participate.

The other area we emphasize when helping people develop a point of view is reflection. Successful executives often have great difficulty taking time out to think about their beliefs. They are busy and so locked into their calendars or schedules that they are unable to step back and roll these tough questions through their minds:

- Do I think that the way we're operating is right from a results standpoint but wrong from an ethical or people perspective?

- Is our traditional way of doing things out of synch with developments in the marketplace, including new technologies and business models that are clearly more effective?

- Do I feel comfortable working in this culture, given its norms and values?

- Am I agreeing with my boss in meetings because I really believe in his ideas or because he's the boss?

- Am I holding back suggestions and making decisions based on what I know will be approved or because I believe they are the right things to do?

- Am I really spending my time and energy on activities that I believe will grow this company and produce results, or merely fulfilling the expectations others hold about what I should be doing in this role?
- What would I do if this were my company?

Many times, these questions can't be answered in the seconds between phone calls. They require a sustained period of uninterrupted thought. In fact, they may require a series of reflection periods over the course of days, weeks, or months. Leaders who grant themselves this time apart are the ones most likely to formulate and express a strong point of view.

Finally, organizations must be aware that people often formulate points of view in two ways. Most leaders today are familiar with the Myers-Briggs Type Indicator, one of the most widely used personality inventories in the world. In MBTI typology, there are two predominant ways people process information and make decisions. People tend to be either T types (they're analytical and rational) or F types (they use their values and beliefs). The T types form a point of view through analysis and discussion; they are compelled to examine, debate, and defend their ideas, and through these actions, arrive at a conclusion about what is important to them. The F types, on the other hand, apply their beliefs to specific situations and observe the impact on others—on their colleagues, direct reports, customers, and so on. When they see that a proposal or program creates support and excitement among people, they then become more cognitive and figure out what has created such a strong following.

The problem is that the T types have a limited impact because F types think their points of view are cold and dispassionate, lacking concern for people issues. The F types are similarly limited because they can't explain in clear, logical terms to T types why their point of view makes sense.

Organizations, therefore, must encourage the development of whole leaders who can explain their perspectives logically and in compelling human terms. Or to put it another way, companies need leaders who can make a courtroom-tight argument for their view-point but also communicate it with the eloquent passion of an attorney who believes in his client's innocence.

◆ ◆ ◆

Chapter Seven begins "Part Three: Heart Leadership"—that is, how we can bring our own feelings and emotions to bear on our business decisions—profitably.

# Part Three

# HEART LEADERSHIP

# 7

# BALANCING PEOPLE NEEDS WITH BUSINESS REQUIREMENTS

## Touching All the Bases

It takes heart to achieve a balance between people needs and business needs. The classic leader—the driving, numbers-oriented, competitive, goal-focused person—never achieves it. A leader like this too often fails to see the connection between growing people and growing the business. Consequently, this type of executive may meet short-term business requirements but fail to sustain top performance over the long term. Ultimately, this single-minded focus on results will erode a company's morale, leading to turnover, a lack of enthusiasm, and failure to gain true commitment to the business. This type of "heartless" leader discovers that if you drive people relentlessly, you'll drive down their effort or drive them away from the organization.

At the same time, the leader who is *all* heart can't achieve this balance either. In fact, if you're only concerned with satisfying people's needs, you may end up with a very happy team who will soon be working for your successor. We're exaggerating, of course, but only a bit. As one of our colleagues put it, "If your main focus is being empathetic, you soon won't have anyone to receive your empathy."

Every day leaders face hard choices between people and business. Should they freeze hiring now in order to increase the odds that people will keep their jobs next year? Should they level with talented but flawed people and insist they work on their derailers and risk losing that talent to competitors? Should they put a promising young talent in an assignment that a less promising, older, more prepared person expects?

These are tough issues that require guts to confront. Let's start out by looking at the compelling reasons to show a little heart in the face of overwhelming pressure for results.

## Make the Heart-Results Connection

We don't have to tell you about the ever-increasing pressure on leaders to deliver improved performance each and every quarter. Jack Groppel, of LGE Systems has written an excellent book, *The Corporate Athlete*, describing the performance pressure that business leaders confront. Jack has studied the mental, physical, and emotional demands placed on leaders in business and compared them to the demands placed on professional athletes. He has demonstrated that the pressures facing the corporate athlete are relentless and never-ending. Unlike the professional athlete, for the corporate athlete there is no "off season." There aren't endless hours of practice to prepare for a weekly match or game. The pressure is constant, unrelenting, and unremitting, and anyone who ignores this pressure for results does so at his peril. We're not suggesting that focus on results should be ignored but that it sometimes can be leavened with people concerns.

Though it's not always obvious at first glance, the ability to foster inclusiveness and to be empathetic can have a dramatic impact on performance, especially in the long term. For instance, demonstrating real concern to a team member and conveying that you believe in him and trust him can not only reward you with greater commitment but give him the confidence he needs to pursue more innovative solutions to difficult problems. This has been referred to as the Pygmalion Effect, referring to the positive impact that high expectations have on performance. This phenomenon was popularized in the play (which later became a movie), *My Fair Lady*, in which Professor Henry Higgins's high expectations for Eliza Dolittle affected her performance. Research by Robert Rosenthal demonstrated that having high expectations can positively influence performance, whether you're focused on students in a classroom or direct reports who are part of your executive team.

A lot has been written in recent years about emotional intelligence and the connection to a leader's ability to instill enthusiasm, confidence, trust, and optimism among the people in their organizations. The ability to know yourself and connect emotionally to others clearly makes a difference in the ability to lead and influence. Yet many leaders still don't make the connection between people needs and business requirements, because they view them as separate and unrelated. Facing enormous pressure to meet ambitious business goals, some leaders who actually have heart are afraid to display this quality. We have encountered a number of top executives who are concerned that even slight concessions to genuine feeling or concern will have a negative impact on business performance. For instance, they're concerned that if they listen and acknowledge genuine objections to performance expectations, they will be encouraging resistance or risk being perceived as waffling. Many executives respond to those who say, "It can't be done" by saying, "Find a way." Others feel that taking time to coach, or develop, or even listen to others' concern can detract from the importance of maintaining an unrelenting focus on customer sales or service. In many companies there is little margin for error, little time to spend in dialogue, and less time to coach for long-term performance. There are legitimate concerns, perhaps, but consider what happens when heart is *not* displayed and a leader thereby fails to achieve the right balance.

Terry is the CFO of a large division of a global company, and he enjoys a reputation as a brilliant financial strategist, strong communicator, and ethical leader. Terry is also capable of being a compassionate leader, but he rarely lets his compassion surface. His unrelenting focus on short-term results, combined with the messages he receives from the parent organization, results in a mind-set that people are more motivated by fear than anything else. This causes him to engage in whipsawing others. He can be punitive and demeaning when they miss their targets, but he can be warm and friendly when he is pleased with their performance. This Jekyll-and-Hyde personality creates distrust and only reinforces others' belief that results are all that matter to Terry. This is why he is losing his team. Some are seeking transfers elsewhere in the organization, while others are actually leaving the business. Those who remain are exhibiting "malicious compliance" but are emotionally disconnected and losing their energy and creativity. Just as significantly, Terry's peers are not happy with the way Terry operates and the negative effect his approach has on their own organizations. Although the organizational culture endorses toughness and a strong business focus, it also embraces respect for people. Terry is violating this last value, and it is hurting not only his career but his effectiveness.

One of Terry's direct reports is vice president of finance of a country subsidiary in Asia. His comments about Terry's leadership style are worth noting:

> As part of our effort to improve performance across our entire region, we gave up a portion of our budget to help fund advertising in countries where performance needed a boost. We did this willingly, since we recognize that the better the entire Asian region does, the better it will be for all of us. But when Terry visits our offices, he forgets that we're working with fewer resources than we enjoyed in the past. This isn't an excuse, but his lack of empathy and understanding of what we're up against and his tendency to blame us for conditions he helped create are demoralizing to our entire organization.

It's important to note that what this VP was looking for was understanding, not an excuse to be let off the hook for not delivering results. Ironically, Terry's inability to empathize undermined the very outcome he was looking for: better results!

A. J. Lafley, the CEO and chairman of Procter & Gamble, is an example of someone who grasps the people-results connection.

In his tenure at P&G, Lafley has been properly lauded for leading the transition from a staid, status-quo-preserving organization to one that is innovative and forward-looking. A dynamic, aggressive leader who has delivered great results consistently, Lafley is usually referred to as "low key" and "unassuming." Kevin Roberts, CEO of ad agency Saatchi & Saatchi, described Lafley as "humble but confident, soft yet tough. He listens, but he's decisive." And Lafley himself has said, "I care about touching people in ways that make their lives better." This caring, heart-oriented leader is also capable of doing whatever is necessary to meet goals. Though Lafley seems devoted to his people, he was also able to authorize reducing P&G's ranks by 9,600 employees to reduce costs, and when P&G bought Clairol, they closed three of their plants and got rid of 750 jobs.

Clearly, Lafley works hard at maintaining the difficult balance between people and results. No doubt, he grasps the benefits of maintaining this balance: sustainability, innovation, and networking.

## Sustainability

As we suggested earlier, companies can survive and even thrive while focusing exclusively on short-term business outcomes, but long-term problems cannot be avoided. To build institutional capacity—to grow talent, to keep the majority of A-players, to create an environment where people work with diligence, enthusiasm, and creativity—organizations must make a credible effort to meet people's needs. A significant amount of research has been done on this subject, and it seems clear that people who don't feel valued leave companies far more readily than those who do. Similarly, leaders who foster a sense of community generate greater commitment and creativity on the part of their people.

This effect is not created immediately. It can take months for supervisors to build relationships with their direct reports, and even after they build strong, trusting relationships, it may be a while before these relationships translate into performance. Time and again, however, we have seen how supervisors who connect with their direct reports are able to develop them to higher performance levels that exceed the norm. Conversely, we have seen aloof, detached, and controlled leaders who are able to demand and receive strong performances from their people for a short period of time but are unable to sustain consistent performance over the long run. Nowhere is this more true than in executive committees at the top of companies, in which lack of community and real concern for each other is reflected throughout the entire system. We have seen dysfunctional teams at the top who are surprised when they discover that their own problems are mirrored throughout lower levels in the organization.

## Innovation

Innovation continues to be the Holy Grail for most businesses—as desirable as it is elusive. Innovation is the lifeblood of any organization, and large bureaucratic systems tend to unintentionally encourage conformity over creativity, risk-avoidance over growth, and consistency over creativity. Innovation is the lifeblood of organizations because it results in new ways to do things—ways that are faster and cheaper than more traditional ones. Frequently, establishing new ways of doing things within bureaucracies requires energy and a relentless passion for change.

If people's emotional needs are unmet, however, they will lack the motivation and freedom to be innovative, at least in most cases. A recent article in the *Harvard Business Review* by Richard Florida and Jim Goodnight, called "Managing for Creativity," makes this point. They describe the importance of keeping creative talent engaged and intellectually challenged. When leaders create an environment of inclusion and support, people are much more willing to speak up, challenge the conventional way of doing things, and take real risks, knowing that even if they must face the consequences of failure, they will continue to be valued members of the team. When employees feel they will still be appreciated and rewarded, even if they make some mistakes, they will more readily suggest ideas that truly challenge established practice. Nothing stifles creativity and innovation more quickly than a culture of fear and risk-aversion. You cannot order someone to be creative; no one is inspired to push for change when he is afraid to fail or is under constant, withering pressure to meet immediate objectives.

## Networking

More goals are accomplished through connectivity among groups (versus individual effort) than ever before. Most companies have defined processes that require lateral communication and informal networks, as well as more formal teams. These lateral networks are responsible for doing tremendous amounts of organizational work. It is much more difficult to drive lateral teams than it is to drive individuals. When team members feel exploited, unappreciated, or bullied, they disengage from the lateral network and seek others with whom to collaborate. It is easier to hide mediocre performance or disengagement within a team or lateral network than it is when there is a one-on-one relationship between supervisor and direct report.

Patrick Lencioni, in *The Five Dysfunctions of a Team*, demonstrates what happens when a team's needs aren't met. In his fable, he shows that when team members are distrustful, they hold back information and ideas. When they don't speak up, they avoid conflict rather than resolve it. When the members don't resolve their differences, they fail to commit to team decisions. And those are only the first three dysfunctions! Our point is that people needs must be addressed, or teams and other groups are likely to become dysfunctional.

## Being Nice Versus Being Kind

Organizations tend to oversimplify the notion of people needs, and this results in making token gestures rather than meeting key human requirements. One of the most common oversimplifications is that a leader meets people needs by being nice. Consider, though, the difference between "nice" and "kind." If you are unaware that you have a noticeable spot on your tie and someone is nice, she doesn't mention it, thus saving you from minor embarrassment. If someone is kind, however, he pulls you aside, tells you that you have a spot and that you might want to change your tie. He is acting in your best interests and, most likely, telling you something that you wanted to know.

In the latter instance, a positive outcome is achieved that would not have been possible just by being nice. Meeting people needs, then, involves more than being pleasant to direct reports or avoiding conflict and confrontation by being polite. It is not just an attitude but an action. In fact, you can only balance people needs and business requirements with meaningful actions.

In many strongly matrixed organizations such as Nike and P&G, there are frequent and intense discussions about how to manage globally. At Nike, senior executives continuously balance the demands of global product standards and local country requirements. In matrix organizations, the potential for real conflict always exists, since strong leaders have strong opinions about organization and come from different perspectives on it. At Nike the senior team is able to deal effectively with their differences, debate them without rancor or accusation, and arrive at annual plans and goals. They are able to do so because Nike has created a culture in which "being on the team" is a cultural value. At all levels, Nike leaders realize it is impossible for an individual to win without the team winning as well. This approach is the foundation of an effective matrix organization in which interdependence and conflict are inevitable.

At Nike, Bank of America, Colgate, Johnson & Johnson, and many other interdependent organizations we work with, the senior team makes the commitment to respect each other, even when they disagree. Many times, executive team members don't make this commitment. They are so cognitively focused that they attempt to out-argue each other. Their arguments are often brilliantly well-reasoned, and you listen to one leader and nod your head in agreement, then you listen to the next person who has the opposite point of view and nod your head again. Soon, the team is lost in a maze of point and counterpoint that passes for dialogue and problem solving. It is only when they display heart—when they allow themselves to listen empathetically to another person's viewpoint and display the flexibility that is possible only when you trust others— that issues are resolved and plans are ratified and implemented, which is then reflected in performance.

Meeting people needs, therefore, can be about showing others genuine respect through active listening and being willing to adapt a strongly held position.

Sometimes, of course, the balancing point between people and business is precarious. Most days, leaders struggle with the desire to do the right thing for their employees and for their business. They know it's not "right" to terminate large numbers of people who have made a real commitment to the organization and, often through no fault of their own, must now lose their jobs. But they also know that by not quickly cutting costs, they might be jeopardizing the future survival of the company. They know it may not be "right" to pass over for promotion an individual who demonstrates the values of the organization and is highly committed to improving but is unable to deliver results. To maintain the balance effectively, leaders must continually take actions that on the surface don't seem fair or humanistic.

The most difficult challenge for most leaders is to confront their direct reports about performance issues or to move them out of their jobs. Poor leaders allow mediocre or poor performers to stay in place and damage the organization, simply because they want to be nice. We have worked with many leaders who dread confronting other people with their performance problems. Otherwise strong executives who have the courage to make hard business decisions quake in the face of giving tough feedback. They will avoid the conversation or obfuscate the message. Yet when they finally do have the courageous conversation, they are often surprised at how well it goes. In some cases they find that the other person is actually relieved. Here's another example of the difference between nice and kind. Being nice means avoiding conflict and disingenuously pretending that all is well. Being kind means giving people a message they needed to hear and acting in their best interest. We often ask a leader who is reluctant to give "bad news" if it's really in another person's best interest to keep him from knowing what he needs to know.

An unwillingness to confront suggests a lack of heart. In *Working Without a Net*, Morris Schectman writes that organizations are filled with "caretaking" managers. These are paternalistic or maternalistic types who convince themselves that they really care about their people and demonstrate it by protecting them from losing their jobs or even from criticism. They view their direct reports as "fragile" individuals and don't want to hurt their feelings. Shechtman emphasizes that people are tougher than these caretaking managers believe them to be, that it's cruel rather than kind to allow poor performers to spin their wheels and never confront them with information that might help them learn and grow or find their right level of position.

On a larger scale, we are working with a corporation that is wrestling with a similar set of issues. The executive committee has learned through rigorous assessment and difficult confrontation with data that a number of key executives are competent but not excellent and that for the company to move forward, they will need more excellence in key positions. They have completed the process of feeding back the data, and the CEO has insisted the company begin recruiting outside talent. Working with a search firm, they have identified a number of leaders who would perform at a higher level. The problem is collateral damage. The current executives have been with the company for years, and they have built strong relationships throughout the organization. If they were to be replaced in large numbers, morale would plummet. Such an action might come across as a heartless housecleaning. Equally important, employees upset with the replacement of their bosses would probably lose some of their commitment and energy, affecting performance negatively. Yet this performance will also be negatively affected if poor performers are allowed to remain in place.

There is no simple solution to this dilemma, but being nice while entertaining average or poor performance is not the answer. In this situation, balancing people needs and business requirements may require a gradual and fair transition; it may mean that the company should approach replacing these individuals as a process rather than as a "bloody Monday" event. Perhaps some of the executives can be moved into new roles or developed to the point of higher effectiveness. Perhaps the ones let go will be given severance packages and provided with outplacement assistance. Whatever is done, both people needs and business requirements must be considered as factors rather than viewed as either-or alternatives.

## The Overly Empathetic Trap

Before we talk about how to achieve an effective balance, we need to warn you about what happens when you are overly reliant on a people-sensitive philosophy. Some leaders are known as people persons. They are empathetic, sensitive, motivational, great developers of talent, and genuinely decent people. Their direct reports are intensely loyal and powerfully motivated. In certain situations and certain companies, these leaders are highly effective. Their people orientation, though, can cause them to be ineffective. In fact, it can be a derailer.

A CEO has one member of his executive committee who is not performing and is one of the few females in a company that has had issues with diversity. In fact, her lack of performance in a critical staff function is having an impact on the entire organization. He knows that it is in the best interest of the organization to make a change, and his board is pressuring him to do so. At the same time, he has built a powerful bond with this individual, having worked with her throughout both of their careers.

When she was appointed to her role by his predecessor, her skill set fit the requirements of the role: consolidating resources, establishing metrics, managing performance. Now what is needed is a visionary leader who can take the company to another level. The CEO knows that she is a working mother with an alcoholic husband, is admired and liked by her team, and is stretched in many directions. But despite receiving 360-degree feedback, coaching, and direct messages from her peers, she is unable to rise to the challenge the company is facing.

In this instance, an excessively people-oriented CEO could view this woman as a friend and trusted colleague, and continue to rationalize allowing her to keep her job. He might decide that the function is really peripheral to the core mission of the business. He might decide to invest in more coaching to help her with her performance issues. He might insist that she attend a functional executive program at a prestigious business school. He could convince himself that she is just going through a difficult period and that she'll overcome her performance problems. All the while, her colleagues resent her ineffectiveness and the fact that her favored position with the CEO is preserving her job.

Be aware, therefore, of the following signs of an overly people-focused leader:

- A reluctance to confront poor or ineffective performers; a further reluctance to move them out of their positions when they don't show improvement

- Reflexive rationalizing; explaining in circular logic to others why he is allowing someone to continue doing an ineffective job in ways that are ultimately self-defeating

- Delaying tactics; avoiding confronting or firing an individual by taking token steps to "fix" this person by giving her a new project, providing her with additional resources, or giving her a new set of objectives

- Falling back on the loyalty argument; protecting people who have been with the organization for years because of their loyalty

- The personal excuse; ascribing poor performance to a negative event in an individual's life (problems with a child, divorce, death in the family, and so on) and allowing an inordinate amount of time for this person to return to normal

As we'll see, the balance that we're suggesting can be achieved by leaders who lead primarily with their hearts or their heads, but not if they rely on this primary style exclusively.

## How to Keep People's Requirements in Mind Without Forgetting the Demands of the Business

Contrary to some portrayals in the media, most business executives aren't heartless. There are those who may give that appearance when under intense pressure to produce, but even some of the most demanding, toughest bosses are capable of balancing human with business requirements. The key is using coaching or leadership development to accomplish the following:

- *Acknowledge the reality of competing needs that must be balanced, and don't consistently favor one over the other.* When you see a situation as requiring a choice of one alternative over another versus balancing two equally important alternatives, you run the risk of sacrificing the upside of whatever alternative you reject. If you are aware of the need for balance but always favor one alternative over the other, you will not have much success. Leaders need to develop a mind-set that keeps the idea of balancing competing forces in their consciousness. They need to learn to choose between two equally important stakeholders or demands in a way that meets the needs of each in an alternating pattern, so that both sides have their needs meet in the long term. Successful leaders understand that to sustain long-term performance, an organization must be sensitive and responsive to the needs of its people or it will burn out its most valuable resource.

Providing leaders with feedback certainly helps create an awareness of competing needs and increases objectivity. Few leaders we know take great pride in being described as punitive, disrespectful, or insensitive. But their actions can inadvertently lead to these impressions. Feedback on how they are being perceived can sometimes create sufficient motivation to change the perception that they must not care.

• *Get in touch with their own heart.* One of the reasons some leaders are so unrelenting and hard on others is that they are out of touch with their own emotions or have never really come to terms with their purpose: why they do what they do. Jim Loehr and Tony Schwartz, in *The Power of Full Engagement*, refer to this as the spiritual dimension that underlies all we do. According to Loehr, leaders derive energy and passion from their "spiritual mission," however defined, and to deny this factor is to limit one's energy and effectiveness. Admittedly, figuring out purpose and mission can take time, and frequently leaders only discover what moves them after a major career failure or the loss of an important relationship, or when they confront a major health problem. These types of events, if they lead to reflection on their meaning and implications, can have a profound effect on people's lives. Coaching, too, can help some leaders connect with what really motivates them and help them understand why they don't put enough importance on relationships in all aspects of their lives. Coaching can also help people see how they act without anticipating the implications of their actions on the people who will be most affected by them. It is very difficult to get to know and empathize with others when you don't know yourself.

• *Be capable of pivoting from driving to listening modes.* This capability is counterintuitive for most strong leaders. Driving behavior originates in the head; listening behavior is located in the heart. When you're driving, you say to yourself, "I'm under pressure for results, so I have to drive myself and my people to get them." When you're listening, you say, "When I'm under pressure, I need to listen to others for ideas and options about how we can achieve our goals." Recall the direct report of the executive we described earlier who failed to listen to his people. One of the other comments this direct report made was, "If he would simply join us in a dialogue about our challenges and listen to our ideas, as well as offering his own, it would make an enormous difference in how we felt about him. More important, it would help all of us find the best solution for achieving the results he wants."

Again, driving for results and listening to others are both important. And they are not mutually exclusive. Most strong leaders struggle to listen to others and allow themselves to be affected by what they are hearing when they are under pressure and seeking to achieve aggressive goals. They need to make a concerted effort to use listening as a problem-solving strategy when the situation calls for it.

• *Develop a more complex worldview.* It is surprising that any leader today could fail to recognize the complexity of the world we live in. However, we are often surprised at the simplistic perspectives that really smart leaders have.

Most executives operate out of long-held personal theories about people, motivation, rewards, and performance. One simplistic view is that goals can be achieved through a relentless focus on execution and results when people must tolerate the demands of travel, countless meetings, extreme workloads, and barely realistic performance objectives. In reality, there are physical limits to what people can achieve, and many companies and leaders are approaching those limits. More important, achieving business performance requires more than hard work. Competitive advantage today is more often derived from being creative, networking, soliciting divergent points of view, and fostering a sense of community that generates organizational passion and energy and, in turn, leads to excellence in performance.

Furthermore, many leaders are under the simplistic assumption that the most important motivator for people is compensation. Certainly, people care about how much they are rewarded for what they do. However, every study of employee attitudes in the past two decades shows that what is really important to people is the quality of the environment in which they work. For most people this means how they are treated by their boss and whether or not they see their work as meaningful and contributing to the success of the entire organization.

Leaders can also fall into the trap of thinking that everyone is motivated by the same things or that everyone is motivated by the same things they are. We worked with one leader who was shocked when one of her direct reports turned down a promotion. The promotion would have given this person more responsibility, but it also meant being removed from a job that he loved and relocating to a different part of the country. Our leader would never have thought twice about making these "sacrifices" and couldn't imagine why someone else would. We worked with her to expand her view of what drives people and how she needed to constantly challenge her own assumptions about what people wanted from her and the company.

"Simple-minded" leaders tend to pride themselves on treating everyone the same. This can mean pushing everyone hard or just the opposite: treating everyone with kid gloves. In either case, such an approach fails to appreciate that in an increasingly diverse culture, people expect to be treated as individuals. With some people, clear directives are appreciated and precise expectations are motivating. With others, ambiguity and autonomy are valued, and any effort to place strict boundaries around responsibilities can be demotivating. With some, you can be direct, critical, analytical, brutal, and unsparing, and they will thank you for your clarity. With others, ignoring the feeling dimension of relationships can (figuratively speaking) bruise their commitment and energy. Good leaders become intrigued with the complex task of identifying what makes each individual tick and then developing and motivating them accordingly. By thinking in these complex terms, they will be better able to respond with the right type of heart behavior.

Finally, be aware that all four of these actions take guts. If your organization is dominated by driving, cognitive types, and your culture is similarly inclined, people will be reluctant to consider people needs and business requirements on the same plane or make the effort to listen, as well as drive results. In these cultures, getting in touch with your own heart is viewed as a sign of weakness. If your company is savvy, though, it will recognize and reward leaders who have the courage to display these qualities and to try and balance two seemingly opposite requirements.

◆ ◆ ◆

In the next chapter, we look at trust building—certainly another heart quality, but one that is becoming increasingly critical in horizontally interdependent companies working to deliver integrated solutions to customers on a global basis.

# 8

# DELIVERING INTEGRATED SOLUTIONS THROUGH TRUST

White spaces exist between functions, hierarchical levels, divisions, departments, and geographies. These are no-man's-lands in which responsibility is unclear. More customer and market opportunities than ever before fall into these gaps, and it is easy to miss them or fail to solve problems because leaders treat an organizational structure as a map of proprietary territories. They manage the white spaces only with their heads. For instance, a project falls squarely between the marketing and manufacturing functions, and the marketing vice president seizes control of the project and attempts to dictate what manufacturing does. Or just as problematic, the manufacturing vice president cedes control of the project to marketing and doesn't assign enough resources and support to make the project successful.

At a time when more and more organizations must rely on lateral organization networks and interdependent matrixed structures, white space is proliferating. As it proliferates, uncertainty grows about who is responsible for what and how work will get done. This uncertainty, combined with increasing use of metrics and dashboards to measure output, creates the requirement for new ways of leading and influencing. As decision making is pushed down, and teams and networks take on tasks that used to be accomplished within organizational silos or through individual effort, leaders must learn to do more than direct, reward, push, and monitor performance. The ability to collaborate is at the core of what's required to be successful in the white space. This means developing the mindset and relationship skills to work with others over whom there is no direct authority in order to identify mutually important goals and opportunities.

Collaboration requires at least two important qualities. The first is the ability to understand what the opportunities (or problems) are. In other words, effective leaders need to have the capability to use their heads to analyze what exists in the white space. Second, they need to use their hearts to be able to extend trust to others, especially to those who may not work directly for them. Ideally, establishing the capacity to work across organizational boundaries will not only help achieve short-term objectives but will provide longer-term benefits by creating a culture in which collaboration is the norm rather than the exception. However, this is often easier said than done. Giving up control and trusting others to deliver can involve a certain amount of risk. In short, managing the white spaces can be tricky. To help you understand how to master the trick, let's first look at white-space management from a historical perspective.

## Redefining White Space Over Time

Adam Smith, in *The Wealth of Nations*, pointed out the benefits of organizations being divided into specialized silos, and for about two hundred years, corporations adhered to this structure. Frederick Taylor demonstrated the value of replicable processes, and the complex industrial organization was born and still lives. With the sophistication of computer technology in the seventies and eighties, companies automated routine tasks and greatly increased the speed at which work was delivered from one silo to the next, increasing the importance of the horizontal (as opposed to vertical-hierarchical) movement within organizations. In the eighties, the Japanese automobile industry took this horizontal concept to the next level in the form of just-in-time management and lean manufacturing, and people began paying attention to the "spaces" between organizations and their external environment. The white space of coordination between a manufacturer and its suppliers was managed (partnerships between the two groups sometimes brought the supplier into the factory) and provided companies with a competitive advantage by reducing time and inventory.

Some companies also seized opportunities in the white space with their customers. Again, the Japanese automobile companies mastered this concept earlier than others. Toyota reduced the delivery time of cars from an average of thirty-six days to eighteen days.

In the last ten years, with the exception of supply-chain management, white-space discussions have revolved around internal issues. Integrated customer solutions have made it critical that functions, departments, and teams operate seamlessly; when a design team in New York needs an engineering team in Munich to work on a project for a customer, the transition must go smoothly. Companies like UBS and Bank of America provide their customers with full-service automated banking, which means that when a customer establishes a lending relationship with a commercial banker but indicates that he would like to manage his personal wealth more productively, a smooth handover to a private banker occurs. In other words, the white space between the commercial business unit in St. Louis, which has accumulated the client's personal tax returns, net worth statements, and income, and the private banking business unit that is headquartered in Boston is managed seamlessly to meet the customer's needs. What may seem natural and logical to the customer can be very complicated for a services company, given that large organizations have many different functions, departments, and offices around the world that may need to be coordinated.

In a product-based organization, the white space is different from that in a service-based company. For example, a salesperson sells a product to a customer and guarantees delivery in four weeks. In order to meet that commitment, Production has to be certain that inventory is sufficient to meet demand; Shipping has to ensure that the product actually gets to the customer; Finance must track invoices and secure payment on a timely basis. If the white space between these functions is not coordinated effectively, the salesperson cannot keep his commitment. And more important, the company's left with unhappy customers.

In the twenty-first century, as flat networks become global as well, managing white spaces takes on another dimension. White space not only exists between functions and department but also across geographies around the world. Freightliner, for example—the truck manufacturing division of Daimler Chrysler—is a classic example of the modern, integrated, horizontal, global organization. Engineering is done in Frankfurt and Portland; manufacturing is done in Mexico, Detroit, Sao Paulo, Charlotte, Cleveland, and Charleston. Finance is headquartered in Portland but reports to Frankfurt. The internal coordination of this complex organization requires new skills and leadership ability.

In any company today, if the white space is managed effectively, it can have tremendous benefits. Consider the issue from a research-and-development perspective. It is now possible for engineers in China to be working on a software development project during the day, and when they go to sleep, they pass the work on to colleagues in Palo Alto, who continue to work on it until they leave the office and then forward their work to colleagues in Tel Aviv, who continue the process. In essence, this company is working around the clock. When the white space is well managed, the handoff occurs seamlessly, development time is accelerated, and the company is first to market.

Managing the white spaces today, therefore, is far more complex and ambiguous than ever before. Consider the cultural differences between the Chinese, American, and Israeli development teams; consider the communication problems; consider the potential for conflict between the groups because of the lack of clear lines of responsibility, which are part of every project. If you attempt to manage this white space only with your head, it probably will be handed to you on a platter. If, as a leader, you attempt to overcontrol the process by directing these three teams to work together or if you threaten negative sanctions if they don't and then closely monitor them, they may respond with productive work in the short run, but they will become disengaged, unenthusiastic, and unimaginative. Talented people will simply move on to other opportunities if they don't find the work challenging and rewarding, especially in developing countries where software engineers are in great demand. If, however, you are able to extend trust, create an environment that encourages people to work together, and find ways to motivate and inspire them across boundaries, whether these boundaries are internal, geographic, or cultural, you have what it takes to succeed in the emerging world of complex interdependencies.

## Understanding What Trust Entails and Why Many Leaders Have Trouble with It

Trust is often talked about as having three components: character, competence, and consistency of behavior. For leaders who are able to operate effectively in the white space, this means:

- Providing suppliers with sensitive information based on the belief that they won't "leak" that information to competitors (character)

- Openly sharing trusted clients with colleagues in other units to increase potential business opportunities for the whole enterprise, because you trust their competence to deliver (competence)

- Giving direct reports the freedom to work independently from home because you are sure they will be consistently self-motivated and get the job done wherever they are (consistency of behavior)

The current environment makes it challenging for leaders to create this trust. As companies acquire, combine, and expand over the globe, and as more and more communication becomes virtual, and as demands on people's schedules become greater and greater, maintaining traditional relationships is difficult. The lack of regular, open-ended, face-to-face interaction works against the creation of trust. The personal interactions that help create character, competence, and consistency of behavior are limited.

Creating trust in the white spaces is especially difficult for purely cognitive leaders or for people in cultures that are purely analytical and fact-based. They are so focused on measurement and performance that they ignore the need to inspire commitment among their people or fail to give them the autonomy necessary to do their jobs. They also may become unreasonably focused on short-term, measurable actions, in an effort to manage ambiguity and complexity, and lose sight of what's required to sustain longer-term performance.

At one large pharmaceutical company, a country manager named Bill was surprised to learn that the government in his country abruptly reduced co-pay price support for a top-selling drug by 20 percent. As a result, his business unit had a significant drop in fourth-quarter revenues. John—the executive Bill reported to—confronted Bill publicly for missing his targets. Though Bill explained the government policy change regarding co-pay, John refused to accept this excuse. He continued to hold Bill accountable, questioning his competence and commitment to deliver on a consistent basis regardless of the obstacles encountered. This caused Bill to begin looking for other jobs outside the company. Unfortunately for John, Bill quickly found a new opportunity for a talented leader. John used his head to manage the white spaces between corporate headquarters and the country office, and his failure to use his heart to understand the impact of his actions cost the company the loss of one of its most talented and productive leaders.

People like John, though, often maintain that extending too much trust is a slippery slope to poor performance. They say that as soon as people believe they have an excuse not to meet a commitment, they start rationalizing their poor performance and refuse to hold themselves accountable. They insist that extending trust across the white spaces to suppliers, direct reports, and other functions gives them license to fall short of their goals. More than that, when people fall short, they expect you to understand and empathize rather than hold them accountable!

Some leaders say they trust people but then contradict what they say with what they do. Specifically, they implement indirect control systems. They tell their suppliers that they are partnering with them, but then they monitor every aspect of every interaction, tracking their "partner's" every step. People then begin working to satisfy the controls rather than out of a sense of teamwork or a desire to achieve the ultimate outcome. They insist that they trust others but that they must "verify" by instituting controls. To do otherwise, they maintain, invites people to take advantage of them.

This purely rational approach is not entirely wrong. No one ever wants to be taken advantage of, and sometimes a healthy dose of skepticism is required. Overly trusting bosses can become too compliant and flexible. If they trust people when the evidence is clear that they should not, they are asking for trouble.

Heart, therefore, has to be displayed thoughtfully and situationally when managing the white spaces. It needs to be an option rather than a requirement. The problem, of course, is that in our performance-driven world, many managers are reluctant to display even a hint of heart (trust). They believe that the risks are greater in extending trust than in enforcing controls. However, we have found that in most cases, when leaders trust people the performance payoff is greater than when they rely exclusively on controls. Assuming someone has the right skills for the job, he will ultimately perform well, even if he doesn't get it right the first time. Most people want to do the right thing and hate the idea of letting the boss down if the boss has shown that she cares and has confidence in their ability to deliver.

Certainly, extending trust in the white spaces requires trade-offs and involves a certain amount of risk that a vendor will take advantage of your goodwill or that another function will use your trust for political advantage. Do leaders run the risk that some people will fail them by betraying their trust? Absolutely. However, the trade-off is that extending trust will ultimately build a loyalty among people who can provide years of value to the organization. Erring on the side of trust seems a better risk than imposing unnecessary controls that may lead people to perform in the short term (out of fear) but create long-term burnout.

## Developing the Ability to Manage the White Spaces

Admittedly, it can be difficult to help some leaders incorporate trust into their white-space-management repertoire. Many have been so immersed in rational company cultures and so pressured by time and performance demands that they resist any effort to encourage them to be more trusting, lest they be taken advantage of. Even in flat-matrixed companies, some leaders find it difficult to extend trust when working on teams and in networks. Even without a hierarchical structure with clear lines of responsibility, they feel compelled to control white space between functions and departments rather than manage it. They don't realize that without the hierarchy in place, trust is essential. Leaders who emphasize controls and excessive attention to details can quickly de-motivate people and undermine an organization's ability to succeed.

Despite some leaders' resistance, we have found that many are capable of extending more trust in white-space relationships by practicing some of the techniques described in the next sections.

### Teach Delegation the Trusting Way

Many leaders grow up in organizations where they believe that if they don't do something themselves, it won't get done—or it won't get done the right way (meaning their way). To them, delegation becomes ordering a direct report or a supplier to carry out a task and micromanaging them to ensure that expectations are met. To help them re-learn delegation with trust, the following four-step process is useful:

*Step 1: Set Goals and Boundaries.*  Set goals and boundaries as explicitly as possible, based on what is being delegated. Some leaders are too vague in how they describe an assignment. Others fail to include the boundaries—the parameters within which the assignment should be carried out. In either case, this ambiguity leads to actions that upset leaders, who then withdraw trust. With very specific objectives and boundaries, however, leaders can move forward, assured that people understand what needs to be achieved and what lines they should not cross. When reassured that their people have a good sense of how to go forward, leaders find it easier to let go and trust others to perform.

*Step 2: Allow Freedom.*  Give people the freedom to figure out how to achieve the goals. Taking this step is itself an act of trust. In the white spaces, freedom seems a dangerous thing. People can abuse this freedom, treading on your turf in an effort to meet objectives. The supplier may form a relationship with another company that you haven't approved of in order to secure resources to move forward. As risky as this might seem, freedom also stimulates other people's creativity and initiative—two qualities that are vital in complex, ambiguous situations.

*Step 3: Offer Support.*  Offer support, and combine it with some monitoring. Instead of imposing support, let others know that support is available. It is an act of trust to let other groups determine whether your support is needed. At the same time, monitoring allows you to stay on top of situations. Trust doesn't mean withdrawal. By observing how another department or function is handling a task, you can see whether they are approaching a point of no return—a point where significant damage might be done—and you can intervene with support if they come close to this point.

*Step 4: Recognize and Evaluate Results.*  The cognitive mind-set expects jobs to be done properly and feels that people don't need recognition for what they're expected to do. Within a matrix, where it's less clear what constitutes effective performance, leaders must offer positive feedback when a job has been well done and helpful feedback when it comes up short. This honesty, too, reflects trust in others.

## Guide People Through Vision and Values

It is much easier for people to trust others when they have a clear sense of what they themselves believe in. When leaders have developed their own vision and are in touch with their own values, they tend to be less suspicious or anxious about the individuals with whom they work. In the white spaces between functions, they become more comfortable collaborating with those who come from different backgrounds and have different philosophies about work. When leaders define their own beliefs, they give themselves an inner sense of what work means to them. This makes it easier to trust others because they have created a foundation for doing so. Without a conscious vision and values, people often are insecure and fearful; they are responding to events in the moment, without any guiding principles. Naturally, this makes them distrustful.

Vision and values can be developed through leadership programs, as well as coaching and mentoring, but development is a process rather than something that takes place at one moment in time. Part of the process involves helping leaders reflect on and articulate their beliefs. Too often, people react to events in organizations, making decisions based purely on a particular situation. This can be fine in certain instances, but white-space management often requires more than a situational analysis. How do you make a decision about who should handle a specific project when it falls right in the middle of two functions? You need to get the project done, but you also need to build a long-term, sustainable relationship between the functions. How do you facilitate collaboration between two departments that have a history of competing with one another? How do you communicate the rationale for collaboration within the white space so groups see the short-term and long-term benefits?

Leaders often are also much more trusting in organizations with values-driven cultures. A company such as Johnson & Johnson emphasizes its credo so employees know the principles upon which the company does business. As a result, every leader is well aware of what values must be adhered to when operating in ambiguous or complex environments. In companies such as 3M, GE, Microsoft, Dell, Disney, Nike, and others, a common set of values exists that serves as a guide in the white spaces. Even when people are confused about what to do and how to collaborate, they can always fall back on the strength of the culture and the implicit rules inherent in strong cultures. The ability to do so makes it much easier to trust people from different functions and departments. In these companies, leaders feel much more comfortable delegating important assignments, knowing that the company's vision and values will help steer people in the right direction.

## Finding the Balance in the White Space

The debate over how to manage effectively in ill-defined and nontraditional environments has been going on for a long time. Though now the debate is focused on exploiting opportunities in emerging markets, it has raged in one form or another for years. In 1960, MIT's Douglas McGregor wrote *The Human Side of Enterprise*—a book that discusses "Theory X versus Theory Y" management. According to McGregor, Theory X posits that people will go in the wrong direction unless effective controls are in place. Theory Y suggests that if given the opportunity, people will try to do their best, even if these controls are absent. Although Theory Y has been behind a significant percentage of leadership training, and most organizations agree that you can generate better performance from people through trust and support than through control, Theory X remains a powerful force, especially when the pressure for performance is intense.

We are not advocating either Theory X or Theory Y, but rather, finding the right balance between the two when managing in the white spaces. Too often, managers working in traditional organizations without strong cultural values tend to err on the side of stretch goals and control mechanisms. Failure to balance this tendency with some attention to the needs of the people runs the risk of creating an unsustainable culture. Of course, erring too much on the side of trust can lead to a dilution of performance standards and failure to adequately meet business goals.

From an organizational perspective, this dilemma is most often framed as a choice between too much control (Theory X) and too much flexibility (Theory Y). At different stages in the life of any organization, there needs to be a balance between control and flexibility—performance and innovation.

Our experience suggests that most leaders don't naturally seek balance in white spaces. More often than not, they gravitate toward one side or the other, based on background, personal philosophy, strength of culture, personal style, or the pressure of delivering immediate results. Our point is that there are risks on the extremes of both sides of the continuum and that leaders need to find the right balance for their organization, based on what they are trying to achieve in the long term, as well as the short term. Managing horizontally increasingly demands that managers not only balance the needs inherent in white spaces, but that they also learn to rely on those in other parts of the organization, trusting their judgment and capacity to deliver.

◆ ◆ ◆

This ability to work with and trust others is tested not only by the ambiguity of white spaces between organizational functions, but also by the diversity of cultures among different geographic and organizational units. In the next chapter, we will explore how leading from the heart is necessary to have the empathy and compassion needed to lead people with different backgrounds, values, and beliefs.

# 9

# WORKING WITH AND LEADING PEOPLE FROM DIVERSE CULTURES

## Developing True Empathy

Just as trust helps leaders navigate the white spaces, empathy enables them to travel effectively in diverse cultures. Whether working with a wide-ranging group of colleagues at corporate or leading a project team in China, empathic leaders possess an invaluable capacity to identify with the needs, values, and beliefs of others in a way that communicates understanding and respect for other ways of living. More so today than ever before, leaders are thrust into situations where they must work with and lead people who are different from themselves. To handle these situations from a purely cognitive basis (to explain but never be able to connect emotionally) won't work.

People are smart about heart. They can tell when leaders are faking it, when they are pandering or putting on an act. True empathy, on the other hand, is transparent. Most direct reports can sense whether leaders understand what they are saying and what their concerns are. They feel a connection to people who they believe understand and respect them—one cemented by emotion.

As we'll see, empathy (which is a fundamental component of emotional intelligence) doesn't translate as soft or easy. Some of the toughest leaders we've known have had a fiercely compassionate side, and it has helped them create strong relationships across geographical, age, and ethnic divides. No matter who someone is or where he comes from, he responds positively to a leader who makes an effort to listen, to understand, and to feel what he is feeling. Even if they have different attitudes toward work and come from radically different backgrounds, empathy can establish a common ground. Empathic leaders are able to establish loyalty and long-term commitment, even in this highly transitory age. They are able to get maximum productivity out of all types of people.

How they do so becomes clearer when we define our terms.

## Empathy and Toughness—Not Mutually Exclusive

Too many leaders in organizations feel that they must choose between having empathy and being tough. Under intense pressure for performance, speed to get things done, or fear of getting too close to people, they opt for "tough" and repress what is often an inherent kindness and willingness to listen and empathize. Although they may work well with people who are similar in age, or experience, or outlook (simpatico exists between people who grew up in the same region, or had the same undergraduate experience, or moved up through a function or business unit together), they can be seen as indifferent to those who come from different backgrounds. This view is exacerbated when they fail to show compassion and rely only on their toughness. They end up being identified with only a small segment of their company population.

Having empathy doesn't mean relaxing standards or being a pushover. According to the dictionary definition, the term *empathy* involves putting yourself in another person's shoes so completely that you can "feel what they are feeling." Empathy goes beyond sympathy for the suffering of others, often accompanied by a desire to help the sufferer. Translated into a business context, empathy means going beyond an intellectual recognition of another person's problems or concerns and taking an action that communicates heartfelt understanding. *Understanding* is a key word, in that it is what people most want from their leaders. And understanding does not mean acceptance. This is where many leaders get confused about others' expectations. Most individuals in organizations don't labor under the illusion that their bosses will give in to all or even most of their requests; they don't expect leaders to bend to their whims or even engage in endless dialogue about a particular issue. What they do expect and appreciate, however, is empathetic understanding. When people feel their leaders really "get them," when they believe that leaders appreciate their position, not just intellectually but emotionally, they respond with hard work, commitment, and creativity. Most employees expect leaders to be concerned with both business outcomes and their well-being, and if the latter concern is communicated effectively, they will usually feel included and appreciated. And this leads to greater commitment and loyalty.

There is a lot to be empathic about in a normal work environment. Parents are struggling to balance work and family issues. Colleagues are battling each other for increasingly scarce resources and job promotions. Minorities (ethnic, gender, sexual orientation, age) are attempting to find their place in majority-dominated organizations. In a global organization, the requirement for empathy is even greater as people are transferred to countries with radically different lifestyles and values.

Empathy, of course, comes with a head-and-guts catch. Leaders who are excessively compassionate run the risk of crossing the line. They become so giving and supportive that they sacrifice their personal standards, as well as the standards of the organization. From a head perspective, they should assess where their empathy must end and their demand for performance must begin. From a guts perspective, they may need to show compassion in the face of negative sanctions related to results, or they may need to display the courage to mask their empathy because the overarching need is for performance.

The "compassion conundrum" becomes evident when you think about how people traditionally adjust to jobs in foreign cultures. Some people on expatriate assignments see no need to engage the local culture; they isolate themselves in ghettoes made up of their own countrymen, only mixing with others from their country or from similarly industrialized nations; they isolate themselves from the people and customers of the new country. On the other extreme, they "go native." They not only accept the culture but immerse themselves in it. They take on all the characteristics of their new culture, demonstrating great compassion for the people. But at the same time they run the risk of ignoring their organizational responsibilities and becoming representatives of the country rather than the company.

Ideally, people learn to lead and manage among diverse cultures by leavening their inherent drive for performance with authentic empathy. In essence, they need to learn to balance the forces of yet another paradox by remembering they are both human beings and business executives—that they are responsible to be responsive to colleagues and customers with different values, but they are also responsible to carry out the objectives and represent the values of their company, which at times may conflict with local country needs. Managing this "local-global" paradox often means setting limits on their empathy while not becoming hardened to local concerns.

Determining how much compassion to show can be complicated by many issues. Situationally, there are times when greater compassion is called for. For instance, an employee who has been a great performer for years deserves the benefit of the doubt. If his performance begins to decline, the boss may want to give him some latitude, try to understand what is happening, and be emotionally supportive before confronting him. At the same time, though, if the boss is under tremendous pressure to deliver stretch goals, and there is little room for anyone to miss their targets, he might have to act more quickly than he would like. Under these circumstances, there is little or no slack to cut. In many companies today, this is exactly the situation most leaders find themselves in.

Finally, don't forget that the capacity for demonstrating empathy is an intrinsic quality, and some leaders are more naturally empathic than others. In other words, you can't expect an equal amount of empathy from everyone. Though we believe just about everyone can develop the necessary degree of empathy for most cir-cumstances, some people are going to have to work harder at it than others.

## The Ways Empathy Affects People and Programs

People sometimes take a simplistic view of empathy in the work-place; they see it as nothing more than a way to build relationships. In fact, empathy performs different roles in different settings, and leaders with head, heart, and guts are aware of its ramifications. Here are just a few key points to keep in mind:

• *Monocultural organizations react differently to uncompassionate leaders than multicultural companies.* In a monocultural setting, uncompassionate leaders may earn temporary productivity at the cost of long-term commitment. If it is a company with a legacy of tough, uncompromising, and unsympathetic leaders who create demanding work environments, the lack of empathy may not have any short-term impact. People are used to it. In a cross-cultural set-ting, on the other hand, the risks are much greater. A leader with-out empathy can freeze the organization within months. For instance, let's say you are asked to lead a twelve-month market study in Thailand, and in your haste to meet the company's expec-tations, you convey that you have little time to really understand or appreciate the Thai culture. Very quickly, your Thai colleagues will disconnect (either passively or actively). People will indirectly com-plain to others in their functional network, and your impact will be limited. You may get the job finished, but you will not maximize your impact or build more influence in the company because you have not shown any sensitivity to or appreciation of the cultural context in which you have been operating.

• *Succession demands empathy.* Empathy doesn't usually enter into a leader's thinking when it comes to succession. Often succes-sion is viewed purely from the head, meaning that leaders see the process in analytical terms that result in a dispassionate assessment of people's capabilities to move up the ladder. In organizations today, however, smart leaders know that they're not just filling an empty chair but replacing a real, live human being who may have established strong, long-term relationships with the people they will be supervising. To disregard this fact, especially in a diverse workplace, can hurt both an individual's career and the organization he works for.

Frequently today, a new leader assumes responsibility from a former leader, who may have been a woman, minority, or older employee. In many cases, a successful predecessor has created a strong team of people who may be very different from the new leader. The team may have difficulty accepting this new leader simply because he is different. If the new leader in any way denigrates the decisions and approaches of his predecessor during his transition or fails to acknowledge his predecessor's accomplishments, he may be viewed as heartless, at least in the sense that he is failing to recognize meaningful relationships that existed before he arrived on the scene. We have seen many new leaders enter difficult situations and be described as "not getting it," usually because of insensitive early moves that ignored the impact of the leadership changes on the emotions of the team.

Unfortunately, the impulse of many strongly cognitive, analytical leaders is to focus purely on the business and work hard to distance themselves from the previous regime. This is especially true when they are replacing someone who failed. They want to separate themselves from that failure and differentiate their approach. Although it is reasonable and desirable to expect leaders to establish their own identity and style of leadership, they also should display empathy, not only for the person they're succeeding but for the people who remain. By showing empathy for what the predecessor tried to do, even if he failed, leaders communicate that they value relationships.

• *Agreement isn't the same as empathy.* When we coach leaders to be more empathic, they often think this means we're asking them to be more agreeable. When they receive feedback indicating that people don't feel understood, they start focusing on being more agreeable and less contentious. This isn't empathy. It is an attempt to be ingratiating—an attempt that always fails. It is especially awkward when an older male leader tries to talk the language of a younger direct report or tells a colleague who is from a different culture or country about all the things they have in common. This approach has no credibility. Smoothing out differences of opinion or style isn't the point. Compromising your values or ideas to achieve artificial consensus isn't compassion.

True empathy boils down to making a consistent effort to understand others and communicating that understanding through words and actions. This means listening to opposing points of view without judgment and engaging in conversations with others about differences in opinion. It also means acknowledging another point of view through small gestures. Perhaps a leader's insistence on starting meetings at 7:30 A.M. challenges younger parents on his staff, who need a later start to get their children to day care or elementary school. A nod in their direction need not compromise his belief that early-morning meetings work best. A recent MIT study looked at what factors affect whether field organizations accept headquarter decisions and positions. The researchers discovered that one predictor was the field organization's belief that those at headquarters who made the decision understood the local situation and the conditions in the field. If this condition is met, those in the field will usually accept a headquarters decision, even if they don't agree with it. To people working in the field, this understanding represents empathic leadership; headquarters must be seen as caring about those in the field and having the capacity to empathize with their circumstances.

• *Performance at any price can have a significant price*. We have worked with performance-driven organizations where *compassion* is a dirty word. These organizational cultures make it difficult for a leader to demonstrate any degree of empathy or understanding, if they believe it comes at the expense of driving for results. Instead, people are expected to "take the hill" no matter what, even if this means pursuing unreasonable goals or doing things in an unreasonable amount of time. Sometimes this is called "lean stretch," or "hairy audacious goals, " or just "the impossible." In fact, a leader at one of these companies was very frank about its myopic attitude toward execution: "This isn't the place for everyone. If you want to work in a more humanistic culture, a more balanced environment, then you probably should look for work elsewhere." Today, many global corporations compare themselves to competing in the Olympics. Leaders take pride in reminding people that they have chosen to compete at the Olympian level and should therefore be expected to routinely deliver the seemingly impossible.

Although there aren't a huge number of these types of companies, there are enough that no leader should be under the illusion that empathy is acceptable or desirable everywhere. Leaders who thrive in these environments are so driven and demanding, both of themselves and others, that they wouldn't be happy in a culture where compassion is a norm. The benefit, of course, can be superior performance in the short term because all attention is focused on results.

The dark side of a non-empathic culture, though, is that leaders restrict their access to readily available and important information. We worked with a top executive at a large, performance-driven organization, who was unable to warn his boss that a critical project was going off track. The company stood to lose $600 million, amortized over ten years, if they continued on course. To communicate this information to his boss would have been akin to saying, "We can't reach our goals here; we should cut our losses when we have the opportunity and admit that it's not going to work." However, the company's culture would not tolerate such an admission. If he had raised his concerns, his boss's response would have been some variation on "Find a way to get it done right." So this leader chose, instead, to pretend that it was still possible to achieve the project's goals. He continued to withhold increasingly obvious evidence that would have demonstrated the need to adjust the project. Ultimately and ironically, some performance-at-all-costs cultures sow the seeds of their own demise. By not tolerating failure or explanations of why success can't be achieved, they cut themselves off from valuable information—information that can prevent disasters and provide lessons about what to do the next time. Many significant organizational and institutional failures can be traced to a leader or commanding officer who didn't want to hear the truth and, instead, focused myopically on the goal.

Certainly, situations exist when empathy is a luxury a company can't afford. Crises, survival situations, or environments in which complaining and whining are acceptable ways to avoid work come to mind. But most organizations do not fit this description. In a battle to survive, leaders have to take tough action, including cutting costs, reducing employment, or sacrificing the long term for the short. In these instances, tough decisions have to be made, and short-term compassion isn't possible. Most of the time, however, organizations that succeed are ones that strike a balance between performance and compassion.

## Example of a Uniquely Compassionate Leader

We are not going to suggest that Anita Roddick, founder of the enormously successful The Body Shop, is *the* model that all leaders aspiring to true compassion should follow. Clearly, Roddick's extraordinary compassion, both internally and externally, would be difficult for many CEOs to duplicate. In fact, some might argue that she unbalanced the head, heart, and guts equation because of the amount of time and energy the company has devoted to various causes. At the same time, we want to share this example because Roddick's compassion has not only benefited humankind but her organization.

> Over the years, the U.K.-based The Body Shop has campaigned successfully against scientific testing on animals, created the first on-site child care center in the United Kingdom, and helped launch the

Social Adventure Network—a coalition of progressive companies dedicated to "making business kinder." In fact, Roddick wrote a book titled, A *Revolution in Kindness*.

None of this would have received much notice if The Body Shop had not been so successful. The company's activism struck a nerve with a growing group of consumers in the 1990s who were concerned with the environment and other issues. They wanted to buy products from a company that clearly had the best interests of the world at heart. Just as significantly, very bright, young idealistic executives wanted to work for a company that thought as much of people as of profits.

Clearly, Roddick also had the courage to found and build a company on a radical social rights agenda and the smarts to market this philosophy effectively. Her vision—that a strong niche market existed for products made by a socially responsible company—was not only right on the mark but ahead of her time. The Body Shop has been on the cutting edge of diversity issues, and Roddick has demonstrated an ability for not only leading a diverse group of employees but partnering with all types of socially conscious organizations. In short, Roddick has led with her heart but has received strong assists from her head and guts.

## Developing Compassion

Not everyone has the ability to develop empathy easily. Developing empathy in a young, flexible executive tends to be easier than helping a crusty old veteran show a smidgen of empathy for the first time in his working life. We're not suggesting it's impossible to develop empathy in the latter individual, only that it may take more time and creativity. We have found that one leader requires only a little encouragement and coaching to find a good balance between a performance orientation and empathy, while another leader needs much more outside help and patience before he can strike this balance. Let's look at the different ways leaders develop compassion and what companies can do to facilitate this process:

• *Through life or work experiences.* When people face personal or professional crises, they naturally develop some degree of empathy and compassion. It may be a death in the family or the loss of a treasured job, but whatever it is, they experience others showing compassion toward them, and they appreciate its importance. More than that, enduring a loss or going through a difficult time opens people up. That tough patina they feel is necessary for effective leadership suddenly seems an artifice. They realize that being open and honest in certain situations can build relationships and help others grow and become more effective in their jobs.

We know of one top executive who was widely considered as tough a boss as there was. He drove people relentlessly and refused to accept excuses for failures. Then he had a devastating accident, and his recovery period was long and painful. When he returned to work, he was a different man. He was still tough when he needed to be tough, but he was able to leaven that toughness with compassion for others as the situation dictated. During his recovery, people showed great compassion for him, and he was moved and helped by this expression of feeling. Though he didn't change his entire personality, he was able to access that soft side of himself when necessary. By doing so, he became a whole leader.

We know leaders who tell us that unless a manager has faced significant adversity and failed in some way, they aren't interested in working with him. Their point is especially relevant in an increasingly diverse workplace. Time and again, we have witnessed young, hot-shot managers who have gone straight from top MBA program to top consulting firm to top company, sabotage themselves. As smart and sharp as they are, they are terrible at relating to anyone who doesn't share their background and track record. They don't build strong relationships with veteran employees or small suppliers because they have no compassion for others who have not been as successful as they have been. It is only when these fast-track managers crash once or twice that they explore their own emotions—a part of themselves that they previously ignored. Instead of just managing with their heads, they learn to use their hearts.

• *Through coaching.* One of the big hurdles in coaching leaders who need to become more compassionate is getting them out of the task-versus-emotion mind-set. Many times, leaders hold their empathy back because they fear if they become too emotional in dealing with their people, they will lose sight of the task. They worry that they'll let people slide because they feel sorry for them, and then there will be hell to pay because an objective was missed.

Obviously, there's some truth behind this fear, but leaders can be emotional and still emphasize the task at hand. In coaching, we teach leaders ways in which they can be empathic but still hold people's feet to the fire. We also draw a distinction between understanding and agreement, as discussed previously. And we ask them to recall situations in which someone else's compassion helped them get through a difficult situation. When they are able to visualize how empathy had a positive impact, it becomes less threatening, and they are able to display it with greater facility.

• *Through engagement with all types of people.* It is difficult to display empathy when you confine yourself to a narrow range of interactions. Leaders who only communicate regularly with a small circle of advisers or who segregate themselves within a function are going to have little empathy for those outside these small circles. We urge leaders to force themselves out of their comfort zones and engage with people in different areas from their own. This means attempting to build diverse relationships throughout the organization, taking the time and making the effort to find out what makes other people tick. Leaders become prisoners of their own experience, and they only display empathy for individuals in the same circumstances as their own. A senior male can't relate to a junior female trying to balance work and family issues. An executive who has always worked in the United States can't understand the difficulties that heads of offices in other countries face in terms of obtaining resources and navigating the political process. Therefore, when leaders force themselves to interact on more than a superficial basis with a wide range of colleagues, they naturally become more empathic and compassionate.

◆  ◆  ◆

When leaders force themselves outside their comfort zones, they must be ready to face the fact that they might have some hidden vulnerabilities that could be triggered by the additional stress of new pressures and perspectives. In the next chapter, we will address the affect of personal derailers on leaders who are attempting to operate with more heart.

# 10

# OVERCOMING PERSONAL DERAILERS IN WORKING WITH OTHERS

For a topic that has been as thoroughly discussed as this one, it's surprising that derailers continue to sabotage leaders. Many executives are aware that certain qualities—arrogance, volatility, and perfectionism, to name just three—can diminish their effectiveness if not "managed." Articles and books have been written (including our own *Why CEOs Fail*) that address the phenomenon of derailers. Bob Hogan and his colleagues described research that has pointed to the negative effects of emotions such as distrust, anxiety, irritability, and generally poor emotional adjustment on leadership effectiveness. We have coached and worked with hundreds of top executives around the world and observed how the negative aspects of their personality constitute a big part of their direct reports' environment. It seems reasonable to assume that most leaders have at least thought about this issue.

Perhaps that's the problem. Although many executives think about it, they don't address the subject from a heart perspective. Leaders may be willing to admit that they can be arrogant task masters at times, but their admission is purely cognitive and dispassionate. They don't consider the effects on the people around them. By failing to come to terms with this behavior from an emotional perspective, they don't address the behavior in a deep enough way to manage it effectively. Or to put a slightly different spin on it, they don't reflect on why they act the way they do and how their behavior affects other people and their own overall effectiveness.

Of course, even if they do take this behavior to heart, they must also exhibit the guts to manage it. It takes a great deal of courage to change a behavior that is not all bad; derailers are often the dark side of positive qualities that have helped people achieve a certain measure of success.

As the chapter title suggests, understanding (head), facing up to (heart), and overcoming (guts) are all part of the process. We concentrate next on the "facing up to" aspects, though, because heart is the key to dealing effectively with derailers.

## What Derailers Are and Why They Are Such a Concern for Leaders Today

In *Why CEOs Fail*, we identified eleven derailers that have been uncovered through research and assessment, primarily through the work of psychologist Bob Hogan. The book describes the following derailers in detail: arrogance, melodrama, volatility, excessive caution, habitual distrust, aloofness, mischievousness, eccentricity, passive resistance, perfectionism, and eagerness to please.

These are by no means the only derailers. You may have read other accounts of ways in which leaders can sabotage their own effectiveness. Bill Pasmore, Sydney Finkelstein, David Nadler, and others have written extensively about leadership and CEO failure. Still, the eleven that we listed are generally representative of the most common ways in which personality characteristics can undermine effectiveness.

You probably also understand that these characteristics can often enhance effectiveness in organizations up to a point because of the strengths related to these weaknesses. For example, the perfectionist can be counted on to avoid costly mistakes and ensure high quality, until she focuses so intensively on the details that she loses sight of the big picture; the pleaser often is a master at building strong relationships among his own people, customers, and suppliers, until he finds himself spending way too much time reading the political climate rather than staking out his own point of view;

the volatile leader can spread contagious enthusiasm until his tendency to overreact to small problems leads his people to spend too much time managing his emotions and not enough time on the business. It is only when these qualities are not managed or when they are out-of-awareness that they cause problems.

We should emphasize that these derailers are not on display all the time. In fact, some leaders do a good job of managing their shadow side until a stressful situation acts as a catalyst for the derailer. Under the pressure of deadlines, aggressive financial targets, critical projects, or other situations that create stress, leaders reflexively exhibit derailing behavior because it is their "natural" way of leading. With a deadline fast approaching and pressure being exerted to exceed last year's performance standard, an executive may become so distrustful of others ("They won't work as hard or as skillfully as I will") that he takes on too much and delegates too little, and his group's performance falls short of expectations.

Although everyone has different stress points, leaders are especially vulnerable to derailers today because of the enormous stress everyone experiences. With ever-increasing pressures for improved financial performance, the need to do more with fewer people and the challenges of diversity and global competition, leaders face more daunting challenges than ever before. Every day it seems as if a new crisis emerges. On Monday leaders must make Solomonesque decisions about who is promoted and who is passed over. On Tuesday they must make a results-versus-values choice, deciding whether the potential profit of a move is consistent with the brand. The pressure can cause even the best leaders to become vulnerable to their derailers. With Wall Street analysts examining every move and decision, boards of directors becoming more involved in their businesses and holding them more accountable than ever before, and the media speculating on their future, we've found that CEOs lapse into behavioral patterns without thinking. Because these patterns have helped them achieve significant goals over the course of their careers, and because the behavior patterns are natural manifestations of their personalities, CEOs rely on those patterns when under stress. In their own minds, they may even view the patterns as positives rather than negatives. They act in eccentric ways and believe their uniqueness will stand them in good stead. They are increasingly aloof and convince themselves that they need to keep their distance from other people in order to make objective decisions.

Richard Scrushy, the former CEO of HealthSouth who was accused (though not convicted) of Medicare fraud, is a good example of a leader whose enormous self-confidence and pride helped him build a highly successful company but who, under pressure for increased profitability, may have arrogantly ignored the rules that apply to other CEOs. You would think that someone as smart and savvy as Scrushy would understand the risks to his image in owning several enormous houses, insisting the spotlight was always turned on him during sales meetings, or purchasing a corporate helicopter (reportedly called "Bonus One") around the time HealthSouth stopped giving out bonuses, but derailers can easily cause even the best and the brightest to act in self-defeating ways.

Similarly, Carly Fiorina was a highly charismatic leader who seemed the right choice to turn Hewlett Packard's people-oriented culture into a more performance-driven one. As pressure for improved performance mounted and competition from Dell and IBM intensified, Fiorina's melodramatic and distrustful derailers kicked in. She fired key people. Her relationship with influential journalists became strained, and she alienated members of her own board. No doubt, her skill as a salesperson helped her throughout her career; the drama and excitement she brought to presentations could be tremendously persuasive. Her melodramatic tendencies, however, may have caused her to make decisions that drew attention to her but were not in the best interest of Hewlett Packard.

If Scrushy and Fiorina could have taken a step back and observed how their arrogant and melodramatic behaviors were affecting key people, they might have acted differently and changed their legacies. If they had been willing to reflect on these behavioral patterns and been honest with themselves about how they were getting them into trouble, they may have been able to limit the damage. It is fair to ask why Scrushy and Fiorina, two amazingly bright and accomplished leaders, were seemingly unaware of their derailers. The answer has a lot to do with how corporate cultures—and our culture in general—view the notion of personal weakness and failure.

## The Derailer Paradox

We coach people to understand, accept, and manage their derailers, but the only way you get ahead in many company cultures is by denying your derailers. This paradox presents a challenge for leaders, who often recognize that they have certain traits that tend to get them in trouble but who know that confessing to these weaknesses will forever be held, or even used against them. Any admission of doubt or failure is often held against leaders in competitive companies by demanding, overbearing bosses or by ambitious underlings who are looking for some sign of weakness in their leader so they can take his or her place. Leaders want to be like "five-tool" baseball players: players without flaws who can hit for average, hit for power, steal bases, field their position well, and throw with strength and accuracy. While five-tool players may emerge occasionally, they are rare.

They are even rarer in the organizational world. Everyone has at least one derailer—some pattern of behavior that will diminish his effectiveness when he can least afford it—in a crisis, when confronting a major decision, and so on. The very importance of these situations places stress on a leader, and stress causes derailers to emerge.

We have found that some people, if they are reasonably honest with themselves, will admit to these derailers in private but deny them in public. Or they might cognitively acknowledge their existence but fail to accept the fact that they have a negative impact on others (heart) and require courage to change (guts). In either case, they don't look inward and face the impact of these behavioral patterns and how they manifest themselves in their work lives.

We recognize that it's not just fear of admitting weakness that prevents facing up to and doing something about derailers. People don't want to work for a system that allows failure. They are attracted to organizations that have high standards and where people are driven to succeed. Ambitious high-performers from top MBA programs, especially, love the challenge these cultures present.

What they might not love, however, is that they won't be able to perform to the company's high standards or do what is expected of them. Even the best and the brightest come up short some of the time. Though CEOs and other senior executives in these organizations present a calm, collected image to the world, they too have their derailers, preventing them from delivering the outcomes they promise; they also lead to failures that may get denied to preserve the illusion of perfection.

In a performance-driven culture like Bank of America and in a highly competitive industry where Wall Street is holding their feet to the fire all the time, failure is not an acceptable option. We recently designed a senior executives program for the Bank of America and included in the design a presentation from a highly successful executive who was running a major business unit. While the program continued for two years, this executive's success did not, and in fact he experienced a significant reversal due to market changes, to which he did not react fast enough.

We suggested to Bank of America that he continue to present in the program, but instead of analyzing his success, we focus on why he did not succeed. This proposal engendered great debate within the bank about the advisability of having a top person admit to failure. Would his failure be an unintended example to others? Would there be excuses instead of insight? Would someone at a senior level be comfortable owning up to his errors in judgment and execution? Ultimately, the decision was made by the senior executive team to continue to include this executive in the program, because in order to become a true learning organization, the company must have the guts to face, understand, and correct mistakes and failures in order to move forward. The executive changed his message to focus on his mistakes and derailers and became one of the highest-rated presenters in the program. Derailers provide great insight into why a leader fails and what can be done about it.

In collaborative cultures, acknowledging derailers is easier. Sweden has a history of companies with collaborative cultures, and Swedes believe that when things become tough, people must rely on their heart rather than their head or guts. This means, among other things, showing empathy for other people's weaknesses. It also means overcoming failure through communication and introspection. In many American companies, on the other hand, when things get tough, people rely on their head and guts. A leader's reflexive response is to issue directives during a crisis rather than listen and reflect. It is very difficult for this type of leader to acknowledge a derailer in the midst of a crisis. When margins are shrinking and share is falling, everyone talks about how the company needs performance at all costs. During these times, heart is viewed as a luxury and temporarily ignored. If a company has to downsize, it has to downsize, and humanism be damned.

We recognize that there is a time and a place for heart and that at other times, performance takes precedence. What we believe many companies fail to recognize, though, is that heart is a key to sustainable performance, that leaders who refuse to face and manage their derailers ultimately will hurt the company's performance, and that what can be a positive trait in certain circumstances becomes a negative one in others.

No leader can present himself as weak or doubting, but he can wait and watch for those moments when it makes sense to say, "I don't know" or "I made a mistake" and to learn from the experience. We have found that admitting to not having all the answers encourages others to learn, and acknowledging weaknesses, especially those others already perceive, actually makes leaders stronger.

When people admit that they are flawed or have a particular weakness, they become more human and approachable. This is especially true when strong leaders make this admission. It gives others permission to talk to them and admit their own weaknesses and vulnerabilities. Too often, direct reports are scared to be totally honest with their bosses for fear of being criticized for bad decisions or lapses in judgment. As a result, bosses lack a complete picture of a situation and analyze it without a true sense of what is taking place. On the other hand, leaders who are willing to admit failure encourage similar admissions from their people. This doesn't mean they endorse or encourage failure. Instead, it is a realistic admission that sometimes even the best people make mistakes. Being honest about these mistakes and learning from them improves performance over the long term.

Again, the paradox of derailers often prevents this honest admission. In most companies, it often seems that the ones who are promoted are those with the fewest flaws. The problem, of course, is that those who get ahead do have flaws, and they're doubly dangerous because no one knows what they are (in many cases this includes the people themselves), and these individuals aren't attempting to manage them. Even worse, leaders don't know their direct reports' derailers. They may not realize the demoralizing ways their highest performers are actually getting results, or see that their assistant's penchant for mischievous behavior is creating confusion among their team, or appreciate how another individual's volatility has everyone expending more energy to avoid triggering his temper than in coming up with ideas for a new project. When leaders understand their teams' derailers, they can help team members learn to manage them and become more productive.

## Three Ways to Manage Derailers

Achieving the goal that this chapter title suggests—understanding, facing up to, and overcoming derailers—is challenging. Derailers are deep-rooted aspects of personality, and while leaders may understand them, they may also have great difficulty acknowledging and overcoming them. The following suggestions, therefore, are designed to meet the challenge posed by derailers, especially the ones related to the heart. Coming to terms with and learning to manage one's own emotional weaknesses is difficult under any circumstances, but in a macho corporate culture, it is especially problematic. Companies can help their leaders do so, however, if they adopt the following guidelines:

- *Focus attention on the private moment of self-doubt.* It's not enough to analyze a failure cognitively or analytically. It is too easy to intellectualize and rationalize a failure-inducing behavior by saying, "I was a victim of circumstance" or "That's never going to happen again." People need to "get under" their derailers, to find where that moment of self-doubt lives. By identifying a derailer and seeing it for what it is—an ingrained pattern of behavior that often surfaces under stress—leaders can learn to accept it and gain the courage to manage it.

Many times, people need help finding the private moment of self-doubt. They may glimpse it when they are on the road and can't sleep at night in their hotel rooms. The anxiety starts gnawing at them, and they wonder about whether their overly cautious behaviors may be hurting rather than helping the company. This anxiety, though, fades with the first light of day and disappears entirely when they return to their routines.

Good coaches are adept at focusing people on these moments of doubt, when the suppressed shadow side emerges. They can help recreate the late-night, on-the-road feelings people have experienced and encourage reflection on them. Identifying the derailer that resides in these feelings is the hard part. It's tough to get someone to admit that he doesn't have his mood swings under control and they are having an impact on his effectiveness. A good coach, though, can facilitate this process through questions, dialogue, and exercises.

- *Identify the pattern.* People often dismiss their derailing behaviors as functions of a particular moment in time. They attribute losing their temper to a particularly tense negotiation process or their eagerness to please to a particularly demanding boss or customer. Cognitively, they may grasp that their behavior was counterproductive, but they don't see any need to change. It is only when they glimpse this behavior as part of a pattern over which they have some control that they take notice. When they see how they fall into a counterproductive routine in certain situations, they cannot dismiss their derailers so easily.

A coach or some other trusted adviser within an organization is best able to help a leader identify this pattern. At the very least, they should identify the derailing behavior and how it was repeated in situations A, B, and C. Further, they should encourage a leader to explore why he reacted the way he did and how his derailer limited his options. Flexibility is critical these days when it comes to management decision making, and most leaders view themselves as flexible. When they realize that they are locked into one type of response because of their derailer, they are justifiably alarmed. This alarm often prompts the type of reflection and awareness that helps them learn to manage their derailers.

• *Present evidence linking the derailer to a negative work outcome.* It is astonishing how readily leaders rationalize their derailers. They may be aware of their volatility, for instance, and they may even recognize its negative impact on their people, but they tell themselves that even though it has a negative personal impact, it doesn't affect their productivity. In fact, they may even tell themselves that their volatile leadership style is highly motivational, that their sudden mood swings are part of their charismatic leadership style, and that their sudden enthusiasms or tirades are essential to the aura that they've created. This rationalization is common. Organizations tend to see their top people through rose-colored glasses, telling themselves that one executive's arrogance instills confidence in his people and another's aloofness provides him with the space he needs to analyze and make objective decisions.

Therefore, these leaders need to be confronted with data that clearly demonstrate how their derailing behaviors have negative work outcomes. It is only when they grasp how their perfectionism has resulted in four lost business opportunities in five years or how their habitual distrust has alienated key customers that they're willing to take derailers to heart. In other words, they are willing to look inside themselves and recognize that they have a flaw that is diminishing their effectiveness. This recognition is a catalyst for change.

In Kate Ludeman and Eddie Erlandson's article, "Coaching the Alpha Male," the authors point out that as smart and successful as many aggressive and confident male leaders are, these strengths can also be weaknesses: the men can be so domineering that they are difficult to work with, and their typically unemotional style prevents them from inspiring their teams. Ludeman and Erlandson found that the best way to get these alpha males' attention is by presenting them with 360-degree feedback that presents evidence that their style is less effective than they believe. It is this hard evidence of how their "flaws" affect their work performance that motivates them to get in touch with their underlying emotions and start working at changing their behaviors.

Finally, organizations should understand that these three approaches tend to have a greater impact on older leaders than younger ones. When you are younger and brimming with confidence and energy, you are more resistant to admitting that you might have some flaw. Highly successful, fast-track young executives, especially, often have never "hit the wall." They have been racing from one job to the next without encountering obstacles. In our recent book *Leadership Passages*, we wrote that negative life experiences often create the right conditions for real learning. Only when young leaders experience a public failure of some sort are they willing to be coached. Only when they have hit the wall once or twice are they willing to admit that they may have done something wrong that can be attributed to choices they made or failed to make. At this point they are able to get past the cognitive analysis and dismissal of their derailers and deal with the reality that who they are and how they are leading doesn't always work.

◆ ◆ ◆

We have examined the importance of heart in four leadership responsibilities critical to today's organizations:

- Balancing people needs and business requirements
- Developing integrated solutions through trust
- Working with and leading people from diverse cultures
- Overcoming personal derailers in working with others

In each of these heart challenges, we have seen that there also are risks—the risk of overemphasizing our empathy and compassion, the risk of trusting others before they earn it, the risk of working outside our comfort zones and falling prey to our derailers. In the next section, we will examine how leaders develop the "guts" or courage to take the risks necessary to be an effective leader in today's complex and ambiguous world.

# Part Four

# GUTS LEADERSHIP

# 11

# TAKING RISKS WITH LITTLE OR NO DATA

Since this is our first chapter on guts, we need to be very clear about what we mean—and don't mean—when we use this term. The traditional definition, especially when it is applied to business leaders, often relates to toughness. The CEO who doesn't blink when negotiating, who takes chances without second-guessing himself, who aggressively acquires companies and annihilates competitors—this is how many people characterize gutsy leaders.

It is not how we characterize them. Our definition involves doing the right thing, based on the context. There are situations in which people need to do what they believe is right—right for themselves, their team, their customers, their organization—even if they know this action will lead to unpleasant consequences. On the people side, this may mean making decisions that have a negative impact on individuals you work with and care about. On the business side, it may involve making a strategic decision that will change the very nature of the company and have far-reaching ramifications.

"Doing the right thing," however, must be a flexible concept. Courageous leaders become ideologues when they adhere to an absolute definition of what's right. They demonstrate naiveté rather than guts when they believe they—and they alone—know the right thing to do in all situations. These self-righteous leaders are unable to adjust to changes in their environment, ignoring ideas or opinions that fall outside their narrow definition of "right." Instead of displaying courage, they display stubbornness.

Leadership courage is often a matter of vision and values—knowing what you believe and when to act according to these beliefs. This means making decisions that entail some risk, based on beliefs and instinct, rather than relying exclusively on the data. The old engineering-based, fact-driven model of decision making is no longer viable. Let's look at why this is so and how it is possible to make good decisions without being overly reliant on data.

## Why the Data Aren't Enough

Taking risks with little or no data may appear foolish, especially at a time when a growing number of companies subscribe to fact-based decision-making methodologies. We're not suggesting that leaders ignore the facts. Instead, we're pointing out that leaders increasingly find themselves in situations where they don't have time to assemble all the facts. Or the data are ambiguous. We also know that leaders find themselves in situations where the facts tell them to do one thing, but every fiber of their being is encouraging them to do something else. As a result of their many years of experience, their values, and their instinct, they know what the right thing to do is, even though the facts may indicate some other course of action.

These types of situations are increasingly common today. Just about every leader at every level in every industry finds himself a victim of information overload. So much data streams toward him from so many sources that it becomes impossible to sort through all of it. Most executives we work with today receive, on average, over two hundred e-mails a day. Making a decision based on this overwhelming amount of data becomes even more difficult because the data change with lightning speed; the market shifts, disasters strike, brands become tarnished, confidential information is disclosed, regulators intervene, compliance rules change, new technologies emerge, competitors combine, and so on—all working to make today's data obsolete tomorrow. In addition, the timeframes for decision making continue to diminish. Opportunities disappear and problems escalate when leaders delay making a choice. The world is moving so quickly that anyone who insists on commissioning more studies or launching another task force before deciding may be making a mistake—losing time to market for first-competitor advantage.

The environment, too, has become so complex, volatile, ambiguous, and paradoxical that a leader's impulse may be to gather more data in order to sort out the confusing picture he sees. More often than not, more data will not clarify the picture, at least to the point that he wants it clarified. Data can do nothing about a new competitor that emerges because of lowered barriers to entry, or about a pricing decision that will cause investors to look unfavorably on margins and potential for future profitability, or about the downside of a reduction in force that leaves those remaining with the company emotionally disenfranchised, or about negative press attention that emerges during the due diligence period of a new acquisition that could potentially affect future value. In these situations, you can't research what is the right thing to do.

Jack is a top manufacturing executive with one of the world's large corporations, and he was struggling with whether to change a product material formulation; the change would affect the company's major product line. A new technology had produced a synthetic material that was deemed more durable than the existing material, and durability was a key issue. On the other hand, this new material was significantly more costly than the existing one. Adding to the confusion, the company was being criticized by environmental groups because the company was one of the world's largest purchasers of the current material; the plant that made this was located in a developing country and accused of not adhering to pollution control standards. Further, the new synthetic material had been found to have a few quality problems in tests, and though the supplier had promised that these quality problems would be eliminated within the next few months, nothing was guaranteed.

The more Jack studied the problem, the more uncertain he became. Every fact he gathered favoring one decision was quickly counterbalanced by a fact favoring the other choice. He and his team, trained in Six Sigma decision-making tools, used these tools to define potential courses of action. The data were overwhelmingly inconclusive. Finally, Jack called a halt to the data gathering and decided in favor of the new synthetic material. He did so partly based on the facts (he found the polluting issue troublesome) but mostly based on his instinct that this new material was the wave of the future. The facts didn't tell him this as much as his experience and the conversations he had with numerous experts. Jack had a sense that this was the right decision, though he could not prove it based on the data. Jack took a risk, based on intuition, but as we will see, intuition can be a more reliable guide than it might appear to be at first glance.

## Individual and Collective Intuition

We recognize that some people consider intuition to be largely irrelevant, as more companies increasingly adopt Six Sigma and fact-based decision methodologies, but perhaps we can remove the negative connotations of the word *intuition* through a few examples. First, we want you to understand that flying without instruments, that is, without any data or understanding of people issues, is guaranteed to result in a crash. In other words, relying only on guts and ignoring head and heart is perilous. President George W. Bush sometimes seems to fit this model. He is a highly intuitive leader who has used that intuition to achieve success. In some situations, however, he is so reliant on his instinct and so oblivious to facts or how issues affect people that he makes significant blunders. His critics suggest that the war in Iraq is one of those blunders. No doubt, President Bush is convinced that he is doing the right thing, and few would doubt that he has the courage of his convictions. At the same time, he might be a more effective president if he were to counterbalance his instinct with some strong analysis and some empathy.

Therefore, we're not recommending that leaders rely *more* on instinct than on data. Instead, we're suggesting that instinct can be used situationally and with whatever facts exist to arrive at more effective decisions. Consider the way Johnson & Johnson uses what they refer to as collective intuition. Rather than analyze the data and make a unilateral decision, they encourage many voices to participate in the discussion. Because so many voices make themselves heard, the discussion can become a bit chaotic, but as Bill Weldon, chairman and CEO of Johnson & Johnson, has said, sometimes a leader must be able to endure chaos and appreciate it in order to discover the right thing to do. Collective intuition has helped Johnson & Johnson break away from the conventional wisdom about the pharmaceutical industry. In the past the company was criticized by some analysts for not divesting its lower-margin consumer and device businesses and focusing purely on the higher-margin pharmaceutical business. Rather than follow this conventional view, the leaders of Johnson & Johnson engaged in broad dialogue with a number of leaders across a very decentralized organization, coming to the conclusion that a broad portfolio offered the greatest opportunity for both growth and insurance against market shifts. Today, with the outlook for drug prices uncertain and pharmaceutical company stocks trading significantly lower than five years ago, that view has been vindicated, with Johnson & Johnson having higher value due to a broad portfolio of businesses, especially medical devices.

Collective intuition emerges after sustained debate and discussion. When people feel free to share their points of view, to disagree with conventional wisdom, to listen to other ideas and reconceptualize their own, a shared idea or approach eventually emerges. It isn't as "clean" as a decision that flows directly from an analysis of facts, but the latter type of decision is increasingly rare. When facts are flowing at such a rapid rate and in such confusing ways, slow, careful analysis doesn't always work. Collective intuition is a synthesis of evolving opinions over time. It is a process that unfolds in a sometimes haphazard manner, and it is impossible to know when or how the collective intuition will emerge. What Johnson & Johnson and other companies have found, however, is that over time, through dialogue guided by values, a group of people will gain a sense of the right thing to do. As ideas emerge and are debated and discarded, one particular path or position will draw everyone toward it. Based on leaders' values and visions, they will be drawn toward a specific decision that fits with their beliefs.

We should caution you that waiting for collective intuition takes patience. For impatient leaders, this concept is especially challenging. People who have spent years making decisions based on logical analysis and data collection may view collective intuition skeptically. If they sit in on meetings that take place in companies such as Johnson & Johnson, they may hear all the discordant voices initially, wonder if alignment is ever possible, and long for a dictatorial leader. They aren't willing to wait for the voices to blend and speak as one. They don't understand how they can make decisions and take risks without more hard facts.

To these skeptics, we counsel patience. We would also suggest that other methods can be used, along with collective intuition, to make the risks acceptable. For instance, Meg Wheatley wrote a book called *Leadership and the New Science* in which she talked about chaos theory and fractal patterns. Essentially, her thesis was that you need to move to higher ground so that you can look down and see patterns that you would not ordinarily see when you're in the chaotic middle of things. This concept of changing perspective can help you see a trend or market movement that is not rooted in data. Seeing an old problem from a new angle stimulates fresh thinking. Sometimes, leaders travel to another country and view their industry through the eyes of foreigners. In this way, they gain a fresh perspective on their industry's problems and may see new opportunities or fresh problem-solving approaches that were previously invisible. They don't have the facts to support risk-taking moves in pursuit of these new opportunities, but their altered perspective convinces them to trust their intuition and capitalize on the emerging trend they've observed.

Many times, skeptics don't realize that they have relied on intuition to make risky decisions in the past because they haven't labeled it as intuition. For instance, many leaders who have been involved in succession planning refer to the process of reviewing the job specs, the results of candidate interviews, the recommendations of committees, and the ranking of candidates in terms of how well each meets the specs. Ultimately, they choose someone for the job, even though all the procedures and information suggest he is not the best-qualified candidate. They select him, though, because their gut tells them that this person is ready and able to handle it, even though the data may suggest otherwise. More often than not, their gut is right.

Another way of looking at this issue is to see whether leaders are willing to take risks on innovation. When people come up with an original, daring idea in response to a situation, this idea usually is rooted in the imagination rather than in the data. Leaders must decide whether to take a risk on a cutting-edge concept that can't be vetted through data analysis. This can be intimidating, and if a leader doesn't appreciate creativity or people who look at things differently, he won't take the risk.

More than ever before, however, organizations need leaders with this capacity. Although they don't need leaders who take foolish risks on off-the-wall schemes, they require top management to know when to take risks and have the guts to back risky-but-breakthrough approaches. What companies need are leaders like Chris Albrecht, the CEO of HBO, who, following both his own instinct and the collective intuition of his colleagues, launched breakthrough original programming with shows like "The Sopranos"—shows that violated many of the rules for television programming and entailed huge risks for the relatively young network. There was absolutely no way that data alone could have told him this risk was justified. Yet there was a collective feeling within the HBO brain trust that this was a risk worth taking.

Sidney Harman, founder and executive chairman of Harman Industries, took a huge risk on innovation. Harman Industries, manufacturers of high-end stereo and audio equipment, made an extremely tough decision in 1996. For years, they had relied on analog systems, but they were aware of the potential for digital systems and wanted to capitalize on that potential. The enormous switching costs, however, seemed prohibitive.

During a meeting with top executives, though, Harman floated the idea of committing all the company's resources to digital. There ensued a meeting that went on for hours, in which executives expressed anxiety and disappointment but also highly creative and cutting-edge concepts. In a *Harvard Business Review* article, Harman expresses what took place: "[there was] concern that we would be betting the company if we went digital. I realized that to provoke the creative thinking we needed, I would have to let my guard down and be willing to embarrass myself by floating unformed—and even uninformed ideas."

What occurred during this meeting was exactly the type of collective intuition we described earlier. They decided to throw their resources into the digital arena, not because the data definitively pointed them in that direction but because the instinctive consensus of the group was to take this risk. This decision has helped Harman's company grow by leaps and bounds and reach almost $3 billion in sales last year.

In the marketing arena, we're seeing a shift toward instinctive risk taking. Increasingly, commercials are airing that have little basis in research. Consider Nike's commercials, which are often aired without extensive focus-group testing or market research. Many of them operate at a level below consciousness. They seem not to be delivering a product message but rather are abstract and mood-focused. Yet they work, branding Nike as hip and in tune with the mind-set of young athletes.

It's no coincidence that Nike makes a concerted effort to develop head, heart, and guts leaders. They tend to promote individuals who possess a good mix of all these qualities, and they make an effort to "loosen up" fact-based leaders by having them interact with designers and other creative types. They seek leaders who can grasp the soul of the Nike brand and combine it with the analytical, fact-based decision making of business experts. Of course, there are many ways to develop the instinct and intuition that allows leaders to take necessary risks.

## How to Encourage People to Rely on Their Instincts as Well as the Data

We recognize that this heading captures a significant development challenge for organizations. Some organizational leaders are inherently risk-avoidant, and they will be reluctant to make a decision that they can't justify with facts. Most leaders, though, are perfectly capable of developing this guts quality. What they need to overcome, however, are the biases and false beliefs that prevent them from relying on collective intuition and their own instincts. Here are three development approaches that will help them clear these hurdles:

• *Connect to people at the margins.* Many executives are prisoners of their own experience. They aren't willing to trust their instinct or their beliefs because they seem irrelevant to the decision-making experiences they've had throughout their careers. They are accustomed to analyzing the data logically, slowly, and thoroughly, and then deciding. This is how everyone they know does it. They need to see that others do it differently before they give themselves permission to transcend the data. In our book, *Unnatural Leadership,* we describe the phenomenon of becoming a prisoner of one's own experience and suggested that leaders don't spend time only with those who see the world the same way.

In most companies today, you'll find green-haired people at the margins. We mean this both literally and figuratively. They may be young people, new hires, or temporary workers, and they can be found in all functions and of all ages. Too often, they're marginalized for the way they ignore traditional practices, pursue idiosyncratic ideas, and believe fiercely in their ideas.

Leaders need to get to know these individuals and explore the way they approach everything from idea creation to decision making. They can do so in many ways, such as joining communities of interest or working on more formal teams made up of people they've never worked with before. In this way, they expand their experience base and discover that there are ways of approaching problems and opportunities other than from a purely head-based perspective.

• *Uncover assumptions about the decisions they make.*  Through coaching fact-based decision makers, we have found that people are often overly reliant on data because they view them as sacred and absolute. When we disabuse them of these notions—when we demonstrate that they are inadvertently taking much worse risks when their decisions are based on false or biased data—their attitude toward trusting their instinct changes. Through feedback and other tools, coaches can help leaders realize that even though they thought all the facts were on the table when they made a decision, a great deal of information was actually missing. Intellectually, most leaders grasp that the information revolution makes it impossible to get your hands on and your mind around all the data. When it comes to specific decisions regarding specific business issues, however, they ignore this truth and persist in using research and analysis as their sole decision-making methodology. Evidence that this methodology isn't foolproof encourages them to explore other methods.

It also helps to point out to leaders that biases based on previous experiences sometimes masquerade as facts. In other words, they are convinced that it is impossible to expand a product line into China because of the bureaucratic restrictions regarding this particular product line; they failed in the past because of the red tape that is part of doing business in China, and they are certain that it will ensnare them if they try to expand into this region again. When a coach helps identify the flaw in this assumption and points out the bias that underlies it, leaders sometimes have a small epiphany about what's wrong with facts-only decisions. At this point they are willing to try trusting instinct and collective intuition and taking the risks these approaches entail.

• *Step out the office and into the world of customers, suppliers, and other "outsiders."* Instinct and intuition are often stifled in homogeneous environments. When people spend all their time in the office studying research reports and charts, they tend to rely reflexively on data to the exclusion of all else. Instinct requires stimuli, and many times these stimuli reside in out-of-the-office experiences. Being with the customer, you develop an instinct for what he needs. Being with suppliers, you develop a sense about how to form a fair partnership. Spending time in a foreign country, you develop intuition about what will and will not fly in this market. Personal interaction with different people and places activates our instincts. Encouraging leaders to place themselves in diverse and unfamiliar situations will help them develop and learn to rely on their beliefs and their gut.

Not too long ago, we were running an executive session for a group of senior executives from a global fashion company. We spent days poring over the consumer-trend data regarding young teenage girls—a key market. Based on these data, it seemed clear what market strategy the company should embark on, including focusing on a modest and professional look for young teen-age girls. We then took this executive group to a Britney Spears concert, and afterwards, we stood outside and observed thirteen-year-old girls with halter tops, belly-button rings, and other styles and behaviors that the research barely described. In addition, the girls were accompanied by their mothers, who were encouraging not only their daughter's appearance but the purchase of that fashion. The next day, we restarted the discussion with this group, and this time, everyone questioned the assumptions of the previous day, including their view of the ultimate consumer and the aspirations of their customers. They began exploring new ideas and approaches that they never would have considered before, and through debate and discussion and a surprising connection with the customer, collective intuition emerged, the strategy was redefined, and the company went on to achieve blockbuster sales the following year.

Taking risks based on vision, values, and instinct is scary, but it is far scarier in this day and age to rely just on the facts. The latter is a much higher-risk approach, since the facts can be as ephemeral as shooting stars. Leaders find it much easier to make courageous choices when they know what they believe in and trust their gut to make the right decision.

◆ ◆ ◆

Making difficult decisions with less than perfect information is just one of today's challenges of courage or guts. When making decisions in a complex world, leaders also must balance short-term risk with longer term rewards and determine how much pressure they can withstand from those who must endure short-term sacrifices. In the next chapter, we will consider the risk-reward paradox of leadership in an aggressive global marketplace.

# 12

# BALANCING RISK AND REWARD

It requires more courage than ever before to balance risk and reward. It can be intimidating for leaders to live in the uncertain space between the two, searching for the right amount of risk to achieve the right reward. Some leaders make the mistake of taking foolish chances that end up having catastrophic financial consequences, especially those who focus only on the upside or minimize the downside in evaluating a course of action. Other leaders make the mistake of becoming overly cautious, refusing to take appropriate risk, and depriving their organizations of significant rewards. Business is inherently risky, probably more so today than ever before. Finding the right balance takes guts, but it also takes head and heart. You need the intellect to recognize the appropriate level of risk for a given situation and the heart to balance how risk will affect the people in your organization.

In the last chapter, we talked about risk relative to decisions without data. This is an important issue, but it is far from the only one involving risk. In fact, in recent years, not only has the level of risk escalated but the types of risk have multiplied. Before discussing the balance between risk and reward, let's look at the new types of risk that have emerged in organizations and what challenges so many leaders today.

## Risk Proliferation

Traditionally, companies have viewed risk from a purely financial perspective. They have also looked at it from a cause-and-effect perspective: the more risk we take, the more money we're likely to make; the less risk we take, the less money we are likely to lose. In reality, risk involves much more than financial issues, and it is also possible that by taking little risk, you could end up losing a lot of money. For example, by refusing to take chances on new-product development or market expansion investments, you can provide competitors with the opening they need to grab some of your market position or cause customers to switch their loyalty, resulting in huge losses.

Therefore, we need to think about risk from a much broader perspective. To help you do so, consider some of the factors that have broadened, intensified, and complicated risk:

• *Wall Street's unrelenting emphasis on performance and growth.* Companies now must attempt to grow on a continuing basis or they will receive negative reviews from analysts for being "stodgy," but if they take bad risks and lose money, they will also be savaged. Sometimes it seems like a no-win situation but one that eliminates companies that cannot consistently and predictably demonstrate both performance and growth.

• *The need to enter less stable or well-known emerging markets.* In the past, new market dynamics mirrored, in many ways, existing markets, and the risks of entering them were lower. For example, throughout the eighties and nineties, many U.S. and Japanese corporations were able to grow by treating the world as a single market, transferring products from one market to another with little risk. Today, because of increased transparency and information flow, a product from one market is not necessarily "new" somewhere else; when introduced, it is immediately associated with all the product reviews and brand characteristics from other places. In addition, many emerging market opportunities are in developing countries, and everything from the volatility of their governments to trade restrictions to unfamiliar cultures increases risk. Of course, failing to enter a rapidly expanding market such as China may mean forsaking what could be the most rewarding new market in the twenty-first century.

• *Increasing regulatory scrutiny.* Sarbanes-Oxley—Senate legislation that was a response to all the corporate scandals in recent years—has certainly changed the regulatory climate. Not only has Sarbanes-Oxley increased the amount of management time and energy required for reviews in public companies, but it makes CEOs, boards, and senior executives more accountable for fraud and other illegal practices. This has created an atmosphere of i-dotting and t-crossing by leaders and directors, since they are at greater personal risk if they put the corporation at greater organizational risk. The requirement of putting a signature on a quarterly attest statement increases awareness of risk and potential punishment.

• *Rising risk management consciousness.* The risk mentality in organizations has spread from the financial function to all areas of the company. Catastrophic financial, reputational, and regulatory risk can now involve anything from an employee's discrimination lawsuit to an environmental decision in a remote part of the world. Risk management is now on everyone's mind, not only in manufacturing companies where environmental and employee and product safety issues are paramount but in service and financial institutions in which a ninety-year-old company like Arthur Andersen can be eliminated almost overnight by the actions of a few people.

• *Interdependence of companies.* Risk can no longer be managed simply by applying internal controls. The interdependent nature of business means that suppliers, customers, and other outside partners can take actions that put your company at risk. Vendors can make a mistake, and you may be a party to the lawsuit filed against them. An outside partner can inadvertently allow information about customers to become public, and you are violating customer privacy.

• *Technology.* Reliance on technology creates all sorts of risks, including vulnerability to hackers and viruses and the need to revamp quickly outmoded systems. Because information now moves around quickly and is stored embedded in computer files for years, the unintended consequences of e-mail exchanges, voice-mail contents, and video-recorded images can appear in a courtroom or a plaintiff's lawsuit.

• *The knowledge management trend.* More so than ever before, a company's most valuable assets are in people's heads. Secret product formulas are less important than an executive's expertise at managing the supply chain. It is obviously much more difficult and more risky to try and manage the risk associated with intangibles. Adding to the problem, people change employers with much more frequency, taking their knowledge to competitors.

As you can see from these factors, risk can be broken down into many categories: organizational risk, personal risk, reputation risk, structural risk, the risk of not taking risks, and so on. Because few of these risks are quantifiable or definable, they must be managed intuitively. As the previous chapter pointed out, this can be a challenge for traditional leaders. They struggle with the risk-reward balance constantly. They want to encourage their people to be daring and innovative, recognizing the importance of maintaining the company's entrepreneurial spirit and fulfilling its growth agenda. At the same time, they don't want their people thinking they are being encouraged to take crazy risks.

Too often, leaders attempt to arrive at some formula or standard operating principle for dealing with the risk-reward equation. Unfortunately, a one-size-fits-all solution doesn't exist. Instead, they need to approach risk-reward issues situationally and creatively.

## The Art of Maintaining an Effective Balance

Managing risk and reward as if it were a science is doomed to failure. Managing as if it were an art is a more appropriate way to think about it. The best leaders today push the edge of the envelope, but they also have a sense of when to push it and how far is too far. They are willing to put it all on the line if a given action jibes with their beliefs, but they sense when it's inappropriate or overly dangerous to do so. These leaders don't just possess courage; they aren't simply daredevils who love to tempt fate. They temper their courage with heart and head qualities. As a result, they manage the balance according to the situations they find themselves in. They recognize that there is no right or perfect solution and that they have to rely on their creativity and instinct—on the art of management rather than the science—to deal with it effectively.

Bob Shaye and Michael Lynne, co-CEOs of New Line Cinema, provide a good example of how this balance can work. They were described as real risk-takers when they took a chance and filmed the three segments of *Lord of the Rings* simultaneously with an unproven director, Peter Jackson. What would happen if the first episode failed at the box office? What would they do with the other two episodes? New Line and its parent, Time Warner, invested over $200 million dollars on the "bet" that *Lord of the Rings* would be a hit. However, Bob and Michael did not simply roll the dice on this movie. They partnered with foreign distributors to minimize the financial risks. So although they did indeed take a big chance on *Lord of the Rings*, they managed the potential downside. In this case they got the balance right and, of course, *Lord of the Rings* turned out to be one of the most successful movies of all time.

Earlier this year, we were working with the CEO of a major company who had only been on the job for six weeks. Very quickly, he realized that his predecessor had avoided reorganizing the company on a regional basis, even though such a reorganization would have saved money and improved performance. This CEO immediately launched an initiative to analyze the feasibility of doing this reorganization, and he discovered why his predecessor had balked: If he reorganized, his experts predicted that the stock price would immediately drop three or four points, and he would be the target of significant criticism—not the way he wanted to begin his job. His experts also pointed out that if he refrained from taking action, not only would they waste money and be unable to improve performance, but they would probably lose considerable market share within two years.

This CEO asked us what we would recommend. Our response: "We have no idea."

Actually, we did have an idea, just not the either-or choice the CEO wanted to hear. To deal with the personal and organizational risk of reorganizing the company and the potential reward of improved performance, cost-savings, and market share, this CEO needed to adopt a trusting, transparent leadership style that stimulated the sort of discussions and ideas that can produce effective "balance" strategies. What he needed to do was open up the dialogue among his key people to determine ways in which the company could effectively balance, rather than choose, the competing alternatives.

Too often, when faced with these terribly difficult balance issues, organizational discussions become black-or-white debates. Some people weigh in on the side of reorganizing; others vote for maintaining the status quo, and the CEO has to choose. Other alternatives exist, but they won't emerge if the organizational climate isn't conducive to open dialogues. Many companies have "speak-up" problems: people are afraid to speak up for fear of being ridiculed or punished (from a career standpoint) for voicing unpopular views or delivering bad news. Some cultures mitigate against the articulation of incomplete thoughts. A boss might say, for example, "Don't talk about that until you've thought it through, analyzed and researched it, and come up with a feasible plan for implementation." Incomplete thoughts, though, are where ideas for managing the balance come from. They are creative, instinctive thoughts that may provide an option to the either-or scenarios.

In many companies, especially in the past, leaders tended to focus on minimizing risk first and dealing with rewards as a separate issue. In other words, they would surface worst-case scenarios and strategize how to prevent them from unfolding. Separately, they would examine market expansion strategies, acquisitions, and other ways to increase revenues.

Today, the risk-and-reward analysis should be integrated. As we've pointed out, risk and reward have become so complex and intertwined that one cannot be considered without the other. The conservative strategy may be highly risky, while the cutting-edge approach may produce little reward. As a result, open, intellectually honest discussions must take place that surface the tangled issues surrounding risk and reward. This is the only way leaders can manage the balance creatively and instinctively.

We should add that more often than not, risk and reward are not managed in this way. There are more wrong-headed and wrong-hearted ways of handling this guts issue than we can count, but let us look at some of the more common ones and how to avoid them.

## Wrong Ways to Balance the Equation

As we've suggested, the most obvious ways to unbalance risk and reward are to be overly cautious or overly willing to gamble. Although we still see leaders who adhere to traditionally conservative mind-sets, as well as entrepreneurial, go-for-broke ones, most people understand that finding a balance between risk and reward is essential for effective leadership. The mistakes they make, therefore, are a bit more subtle than the two just mentioned, and they often have to do with too much head and heart and not enough guts.

- *Focusing too narrowly on the interpersonal side of leadership.* Some leaders have too much heart and agonize over people decisions. Many times, they refuse to downsize a bloated workforce because they can't tolerate the pain they are going to cause valued employees. As well-intentioned as this refusal might be, it may also ignore the fact that if they refuse to downsize by a thousand today, they will likely have to downsize two thousand tomorrow. They may also struggle with decisions about individuals: putting the wrong people in key jobs because of friendships or refusing to move a long-time colleague out of a critical position, even though he has displayed an inability to do the job effectively. All this places the organization at much greater risk, as mediocrity and incompetence is institutionalized.

- *Attempting to quantify all risk.* This is the head approach, and it treats the risk-reward equation as something that can be calculated. Actually, the goal is to control all risk in order to maintain a certain level of reward, and this is impossible in a volatile, unpredictable world. Nonetheless, leaders look at problems and opportunities and calculate the odds of different approaches, opting only for the ones where the odds are weighted in their favor. The problem here is not only that it is difficult to calculate the odds with any accuracy but that only backing "sure things" guarantees that innovative and new approaches will be avoided. Consequently, risks are increased and rewards are decreased because at least some cutting-edge approaches are crucial for being competitive in this environment.

• *Segregating risk responsibility with a risk management person or "at the end of the assembly line."* It is difficult for leaders to balance risk and reward when they attempt to encapsulate risk responsibility in one specialist or function. Too often, we see CEOs and other leaders who only want to focus on reward and hate dealing with the complex issues that are part of risk. By washing their hands of risk responsibilities, they send a message to other executives that they can also cordon off risk or only take responsibility for a small piece of the risk issues. Because of this attitude, very little dialogue about risk takes place at the top of companies. People don't have productive conversations that help them understand the risk-reward dynamic in various situations, and, as a result, little insight exists about what is the best risk-reward balance in a given situation.

Joe Berardino, former CEO of Arthur Andersen, makes a similar point about corporate governance and how boards are overly focused on a narrow piece of the value chain and fail to have conversations about organizational management and leadership risks. Although a board may thoroughly discuss financial risks, it doesn't always look at risk in the broader sense of the term and thus doesn't help organizational leadership think in balanced ways about risks and rewards. Berardino also makes the point that leaders have the tendency to get people to sign off on new programs and projects as a way of pushing responsibility for risk downward. By making the person at the end of the assembly line responsible for the risk-reward balance, opportunities for important discussions among senior leaders about risk are limited. No one at the top is examining the risks of moving forward, so little awareness exists of what the real risks are versus the real rewards.

• *Failing to push for total transparency.*  Companies end up taking foolish risks (or not taking good risks) because an air of secrecy surrounds risk-related issues. Leaders are often unwilling to be open about risks; they may cover up mistakes they made in the past that resulted in negative outcomes because they don't want to be accused of having taken bad risks. We have found that the more transparent leaders are, the more they reduce the odds of taking bad risks. With an ongoing dialogue around why one risk didn't pay off and why one did, learning occurs and companies are better able to deal with similar risk-reward scenarios in the future.

• *Maintaining a compliant rather than a committed attitude.*  Risk management has traditionally involved compliance to policies and procedures rather than commitment to the best interest of the company, that is, to finding the right balance between risk and reward. A compliant attitude represents fear of risk and distrust of people. Invariably, compliance-based decisions are designed to seek refuge from risk by following the rules. In this way, if something goes wrong, people can always justify their actions by pointing to the rules they followed. Commitment, on the other hand, means examining each risk-reward scenario with larger organizational goals in mind. In this way, leaders aren't bound by policies and procedures but can consider what decision is in the best interest of the company, both today and tomorrow. By being committed to the company's best interest, leaders evaluate situations on a case-by-case basis and don't look for excuses when things go awry.

## Creating a Climate and Leaders Who Know How to Balance Paradoxical Situations

As we noted earlier, balancing risk and reward is an art, not a science. As a result, you can't tell people how to do it. What you can and should do, however, is come at this issue from a number of different directions, giving people the opportunity to think about the balance, to reflect on the human issues involved, and to develop the courage necessary to maintain the balance rather than become overly conservative at the first sign of trouble. Here are some diverse ways to develop leaders' abilities in this area:

• *Provide a forum for risk-reward storytelling.* We recently held a forum for UBS leaders in Switzerland that focused on trust, and as part of the forum participants talked about how they had learned to react in different ways to risk and reward. They described both effective and ineffective reactions, and they helped other participants start thinking and talking about their own risk-reward issues. These dialogues are essential. Without them, key issues aren't discussed or are only addressed superficially.

In most companies, the top people lack the time to deal with the risk-reward questions of their people. They are running from meeting to meeting and are under a great deal of pressure because of other issues. As a result, they fail to answer their people's questions about risks and rewards or help them learn how to navigate this tricky paradox. Organizations need to create a climate where there's greater awareness of how to balance risk and reward. An ongoing dialogue needs to take place, so that people can come to terms with how they're going to deal with risk and reward, and the best way to catalyze this discussion is by having other leaders share stories of grappling with this difficult balance.

• *Wake people up to their own derailing behaviors.* Being overly cautious is the derailer most likely to cause a leader to unbalance the risk-reward equation. Many times, though, people don't realize that this is a derailer or that they've fostered an atmosphere where people are afraid to take risks. One wake-up call involves a team climate survey. As part of this survey, team members are asked whether they feel as if they can speak their minds, if there is a free flow of ideas, and if they believe they have the freedom to take risks when necessary. It's surprising how many times leaders are surprised by the results of these surveys. Leadership believes they have created a climate in which intelligent risk-taking is encouraged, but they discover that their team feels very differently. The wake-up call helps people become aware that they are sending messages of risk avoidance, and it makes them conscious of specific ways in which they're doing so. Ideally, this increased consciousness encourages them to take the actions necessary to create a climate that is more open and transparent.

• *Take actions that encourage people to take more heart-related risks.* Some leaders are absolutely unwilling to do anything that might "hurt" their people or damage their relationships with colleagues or direct reports. Consequently, they refuse to take relationship risks, even if significant rewards are possible if they take those risks. For instance, by moving responsibility for a key project from a long-time direct report to a younger, more aggressive new hire, a leader may be able to increase the odds that the project will be completed effectively and on time. The risk is that he may alienate the long-time employee, who feels slighted because he was bypassed for the project.

We would be the last people to advocate ignoring relationship issues, but we know that some leaders struggle with these issues. To help these individuals rebalance the risk-reward equation, consider the "Take your three best people and move them" exercise. This involves talking to the risk-averse leader about what might happen if he were to move his three best people out of his group. By asking him questions and exploring scenarios involving this radical action, this leader may start to understand that keeping people happy at all costs can be counterproductive. During these discussions, we often help leaders realize that their best people will likely leave their groups sooner or later; their talent will naturally attract other offers and opportunities.

This type of exercise may help people grasp that their fears about people risks have been exaggerated, that they need to take some chances in this area in order to improve performance.

- *Avoid template management.* As companies become more global, template management becomes a common reflex that reduces leaders' ability to take risks. Templates emerge from global and regional offices as a way to standardize selling policies, impose quality control on product manufacturing, and squeeze out every possible drop of productivity. A side effect of these templates is to create rigid controls that limit options for managers, especially in the area of risk. If they attempt to implement a cutting-edge concept or try something that falls outside the company protocols, they will stand in violation of the rules. Although templates may be effective in controlling costs in the short term, they also end up controlling risk, and this has a negative long-term impact on rewards.

- *Encourage greater self-awareness.* Managing the risk-reward balance effectively is difficult if leaders are unaware of their strengths and weaknesses, motivations and biases. When a situation makes them extremely anxious because of their particular weakness, they become illogically conservative and refuse to take risks. When a situation triggers their derailer, they may throw caution to the winds and move aggressively forward, ignoring the danger.

Foolish courage is as dangerous as no courage when it comes to the risk-reward balance. Leaders are most likely to act in foolhardy or extremely conservative ways when they are at the mercy of their weaknesses and biases. For instance, they aren't aware that their arrogance is causing them to take a gamble on a project that has a relatively small upside and a relatively large downside. They are driven to prove they are right, even though proof requires a huge, unreasonable risk.

Through coaching and other methods, leaders can get to know themselves better, and that knowledge will increase the odds that they can manage risk and reward, based on their experiences and instinct, without unaddressed or submerged personal issues getting in the way.

◆ ◆ ◆

In the end, however, the most important part of leading with guts is character. Character involves knowing what you stand for and what you are willing to stand up for. It means having a personal set of values that translate into an integrity of purpose that not only undergirds your actions but is transparent and inspiring to others. In the last chapter of guts, we examine personal integrity and its importance in melding head, heart, and guts into effective personal, organizational, and global leadership.

# 13

# ACTING WITH
# UNYIELDING INTEGRITY

It is both more difficult and more necessary than ever before to act with unyielding integrity in today's corporate environment. We live in a time when trust in institutional leaders, especially business leaders, is at an all-time low, due to corporate and accounting scandals that have rocked companies like Enron, Adelphia, Worldcom, Tyco, and Vivendia. Excessive compensation, insider stock trading, and the practice of appointing cronies and friends to key positions or boards have elevated levels of skepticism and distrust of business leaders. People are reflexively cynical about CEOs and other executives, assuming that they are acting with their image and career in mind rather than in accordance with a higher set of values. Complicating matters, the pressure for performance often causes leaders to act pragmatically but not necessarily in ways that are consistent with humanistic, personal values. Leaders may find themselves in situations where they are "forced" to give people false hope about the company's future so they remain productive, even though they know that some of them may not have a job within twelve months.

As difficult as it is to act with integrity, it is absolutely essential to do so. This guts trait is so critical because it creates tremendous positive energy within an organization. In companies where leaders exhibit integrity, a high level of commitment and confidence exists. Leaders with great integrity energize the workforce, demonstrating a commitment to higher principles that is inspirational. In a complex and confusing world, unyielding integrity is something that people understand, relate to, and respect.

The tension between the need to act with integrity and the difficulty of doing so has never been higher, and perhaps the best way to start dealing with this tension is by understanding what "unyielding integrity" really means.

## How Integrity Translates into Leadership Terms

Integrity is not an absolute concept, despite the "unyielding" modifier we placed in front of it. We recognize that integrity, like all the traits we've been discussing, is situational. Although some "absolutists" might disagree, what may constitute integrity for one CEO in one context or culture may be naïve idealism to another. From a leadership perspective, then, we define *integrity* as an evolving set of beliefs that guide people's actions in tough, challenging times. Beliefs foster a sense of doing the right thing and provide leaders with a way to act consistently. They often evolve in response to experiential learning rather than out of corporate statements of values or crass careerism. They are honestly and deeply held but have some "give" to them. As we advise leaders: "Act with unyielding integrity, but don't be stupid about it."

Let us examine some aspects of unyielding integrity, as they manifest themselves in leadership situations:

• *Internal belief can be at odds with external rules or "higher" ideals.* Leaders often face situations when they know what is right but their belief runs counter to what their boss believes, what the organization values, or what customers, economics, or regulatory bodies demand. They also may have a specific personal value that is at odds with a larger principle, as the following example illustrates.

Colin Powell—a man almost universally praised for his principles—has not always agreed with everything President George W. Bush asked him to do, or at least that seems to be the case relative to the decision for the United States to go to war in Iraq. Instead of resigning his position as secretary of state, as someone with a rigid sense of integrity might have done and as many people who opposed the war wanted him to do, he found an alternative path that allowed him, in good conscience, to remain in the Bush administration. No doubt it was not an ideal path, and there probably were times when Powell felt uncomfortable saying and doing certain things. But integrity isn't just about one's own personal beliefs; it can be about a larger set of principles. Powell clearly believes in his country and in serving its commander and chief. We can assume that he believed that duty and commitment to the well-being of the country took precedence over his personal political beliefs. He determined that the best course of action was to stay on the job. At times, it's likely that he had to swallow his pride in order to perform effectively, so you could argue that he showed great integrity by making this sacrifice.

However, another point of view might argue that he diluted his impact as a leader by compromising his personal values. His effectiveness diminished, as it became more obvious that his views were at least somewhat at odds with the people he was being asked to follow. We believe that Colin Powell displayed unyielding integrity by placing the interests of the country first, but other leaders may have made a different choice in the same situation and be seen as equally unyielding.

We use this example to highlight the difficulty and complexity associated with the challenge of acting with integrity. Here are other challenges.

• *Integrity is not always a black-or-white issue.* As the example of Colin Powell demonstrates, integrity is not necessarily a question of choosing between a clearly right and a clearly wrong course of action. Nonetheless, people often make the mistake of perceiving it this way. Any leader who looks at integrity in black-or-white terms is in danger of becoming an ideologue. People who are strongly guided by their heart may believe in always putting people first, but strict adherence to this principle will undermine their ability to succeed or even survive in performance-driven cultures.

As coaches, we sometimes find ourselves hovering in the gray area when it comes to integrity issues. For instance, we're hired to coach an executive. During the course of our work we have many conversations in which we explore her feelings about the company, her boss, and the culture. We also gather information about this person through interviews with her colleagues and direct reports. At some point in our work, the CEO may ask us, "What do you think of this person? What do others think about her?" We don't want to violate the implicit pact we've made with the person we're coaching and reveal confidential information. On the other hand, the CEO is the one who hired us and is paying our fee.

Recognizing that this issue isn't black-and-white, though, goes a long way toward helping us manage it. In this instance, we need to keep the CEO informed about this individual's development and future potential, but we also agree up-front with both the CEO and the executive being coached what information will or will not be shared. Doing the best we can to satisfy both conflicting demands requires integrity.

• *Most people who violate their integrity don't realize they're doing so.* Contrary to the general public's expectations, most CEOs have exceptional integrity. In this age of intense media and regulatory scrutiny and with boards being held accountable for any ethical violations, CEOs are externally motivated to exhibit strong and appropriate values. When they or other leaders in the company act in ways that seem to lack integrity, they are rarely acting out of pure self-interest. Instead, they become caught up in the need to act now, the confusion of the moment, and their own desire to achieve a goal. Only with hindsight do they look back and realize they did something wrong and ask themselves, "Why did I do that? Why wasn't I thinking about this issue then?" One leader we spoke with reminded us that there are really very few people in companies who have evil intentions. However, there are lots of good, well-intentioned people who sometimes make mistakes.

Most leaders are good people who occasionally act badly. The pressure for results, the internal political battles they're waging, the complexity of the issues they are dealing with, and other factors can cloud their judgment. As we pointed out in an earlier chapter, leaders can exhibit derailment behaviors under pressure, which can also interfere with the desire to act with integrity. The arrogant leader, intent on building his reputation and legacy, doesn't realize that he is taking credit for other people's accomplishments; he justifies his actions as necessary for him to consolidate his power and influence. The overly cautious individual invents worst-case scenarios constantly and believes that he can trigger them with even the slightest misstep; he fails to promote a deserving individual, simply because he fears such a move will offend other executives and trigger their resignations.

Since derailers are most likely to emerge under stressful conditions, there are times when leaders are confronted with issues of integrity that they mishandle without even knowing it. Caught up in crises and other stressful situations, they may not be conscious that they are doing something that flies in the face of their own beliefs or that they would never do if they were under less pressure.

• *Integrity requires a process of building and displaying character.* Kevin Cashman, author of *Leadership from the Inside Out*, distinguishes between persona and character as follows: "Persona is acting based on what others expect of you, and character is acting based on what you believe and what you think is right. Integrity, then, is all about character and transparency—letting people see the real you." We should add that in most business environments, incentives exist to disguise rather than reveal character. People who honestly admit to their fears and who candidly speak out when they disagree with the CEO are often seen as cowards or troublemakers. Their integrity becomes a black mark that may be used against them. Many people are aware of this fact and only reluctantly speak up, or they disguise their true agendas and views.

We're not telling leaders to always speak their minds and ignore political considerations. As we noted earlier, we believe you should act with integrity but not be stupid about it. The best leaders, though, pick their spots and establish reputations for acting in a way

that's based on a consistent set of values. Through a series of difficult choices as leaders, they reveal what they're all about. At times,
they must take unpopular stands or risk offending customers and
other top executives. They may choose to issue a statement that
prompts attacks from analysts and the media, even when knowing
full well these attacks are coming. This takes guts—but guts based
on principle. Furthermore, this demonstrates that they are leaders
of character, which in turn can energize their people and garner
respect, even from those who don't approve of their actions.

• *Integrity emerges (or doesn't) during defining moments.* During
"ordinary" moments in the business day, leaders may face decisions
in which they act according to their values, but it is the extraordinary moments that define a leader's integrity. Typically, these
moments are catalyzed by a crisis or seemingly impossible decision.

Joseph Badarraco—a Harvard business professor—has written
an excellent book on this subject titled *Defining Moments*. According to Badaracco, the crucible of character definition occurs at the
moment when one must choose integrity over expediency, stand-
ing out versus fitting in, and choosing a difficult, even penalizing
alternative because one's values require it. Frequently, these situations incorporate "right versus right" alternatives rather than "right
versus wrong." He argues that while penalties might accrue in the
short run, the longer-term task of creating leadership character and
integrity is strengthened by choosing the "more right" alternative
defined by one's values. Here's an example:

> A company is attempting to be seen as embracing diversity after it
> has been on the receiving end of a highly publicized discrimination
> lawsuit. A senior executive in the organization is facing a decision
> about whom to promote to a key position. It comes down to two
> candidates, both of whom this executive feels are qualified. Though
> this executive believes that Candidate A may be the best person for
> the job, he is under considerable pressure to select Candidate B, who
> has less experience but is a minority. Both alternatives are accom-

panied by a logical set of arguments for being the right thing to do. Is he being truly objective? Is he overweighting the criterion of experience? Is it not in the organization's best interest to promote the minority candidate and invest heavily in his development? Whether this executive considers the alternatives deeply and defines his own beliefs, rather than caves in to pressure from others, will determine whether he acts with unyielding integrity.

We recognize that most leaders are under great pressure to bow to external demands, that they may feel an obligation to a boss, customer, or board. This pressure calls to mind three questions that Joe Berardino has borrowed from Jesuit theologians and uses to challenge senior executives around the issue of ethics and integrity: (1) Who are you? (2) Whose are you? and (3) Who are you called to become? The first and third questions are relatively clear to most leaders today. They are called upon to establish a strong identity, leverage their personal strengths and capabilities, and articulate a clear sense of direction. The second question is much more challenging and complex. In most work environments, people feel "owned" in some sense, and it is important for leaders to think through for whom they are actually working and serving. Integrity, then, is the ability to free oneself from that ownership and act independently when the issue is sufficiently important and meaningful.

- *Integrity exists on a continuum.* You can show integrity by pointing out that your reimbursement for a business expense was $10 more than it should have been. You can display integrity by politely disagreeing with another executive in a leadership team meeting. And you can act with integrity when you challenge the CEO because you believe he is not being true to the organization's purpose. Just as it's a mistake to think of this trait as black or white—either you have it or you don't—it's equally ill advised to think every display of integrity is the same.

Think about at least three categories that can describe acts of integrity—those involving the least-to-the-most personal risk:

- *Following the rules.* In this case, a leader pursues a course of action or makes a decision because of written laws, cultural norms, or corporate policies. She knows these laws, norms, and policies are fair, and she has no trouble complying. Actions here are guided by external versus internal standards.

- *Doing what is right without any potential personal risk.* Here, a leader makes a decision that he truly believes in and that may not be easy to make, but if there are negative consequences, they won't affect him significantly. He doesn't risk censure, controversy, or the loss of his job as a consequence of the action.

- *Doing what is right at significant career or job or personal risk.* This is where leaders with true integrity shine and where some of them experience temporary setbacks. Refusing a direct order from a boss or making a decision that contradicts the CEO's agenda can get you fired or prevent you from advancing in your career.

These last types of action can also earn a leader great respect and admiration and, in the right circumstances, even further a career. Taking a risk based on personal beliefs is what unyielding integrity is all about.

## People Who Display the Courage of Their Convictions

We'd like to share with you four stories that communicate what it means when leaders act with unyielding integrity. Too often, we think of integrity in simplistic terms: an executive who resigns in protest over his company's environmental policy or becomes a governmental whistleblower because he can't go along with his company's discriminatory hiring practices. Although these actions may be based on a set of strong beliefs and values, they don't reflect the complex and ambiguous positions in which most leaders find themselves on a day-to-day basis. If a company is doing something that is obviously wrong, such as breaking laws or behaving reprehensibly in the public's eye, most leaders know what to do. Although these situations pose considerable risk, the options are normally very clear, and continuing to tolerate the situation is not one of them. More often, leaders find themselves in far more ambiguous situations where the choices are not so clear-cut.

Each one of the four stories that follow illustrates both the difficulty and the complexity of doing the right thing. The first is a follow-up from an earlier chapter in which we discussed the beloved executive who resigned from his company to spare them the difficulty of having to move him out involuntarily.

### A Leader Resigns Knowing He's Not Right for the Job

This leader had not met critical performance objectives for some time, and his business was in trouble. Furthermore, it was clear to everyone that he was not the person capable of fixing the problems. As someone whose twenty-five years of success with the company had earned him enormous respect and loyalty, he could have made it tough for his company to get rid of him. He might even have successfully made an argument that would have deterred his boss from moving him out.

Instead, because he knew that the company would be better off with a different leader in the job, he did the right thing and resigned. No doubt, this decision was not made easily. Not only did he give up a lucrative job, but he had to swallow his pride. In the end, his strong sense of integrity drove him to do the right thing.

### A Consultant Rejects Lucrative Work

A top consultant with a large firm was approached by a client to assist his organization with a tough corporate culture change. The client was anxious to get started, and he wanted a broad range of programs implemented immediately. These programs would generate a huge amount of income for the consultant's firm, where the firm was eager to become entrenched. Yet the more the consultant thought about it, the more he realized that implementing these programs was premature. He concluded that his client needed to do much more analysis and to create a more sophisticated strategy for the culture change before his capabilities as a consultant could be used effectively.

As difficult as it was to forego the income and to risk incurring the eager client's wrath, this consultant stuck to his belief in what was right. He turned down the work. Though the client was not pleased with this response initially, he came to understand that the consultant had done him a great service; had he moved forward prematurely, a great deal of time and money would have been wasted.

## A CEO Cleans House

Edward Breen, who took over the scandal-plagued Tyco International, has worked miracles with the company's recovery, dramatically reducing its debt and tripling net earnings. What is not widely known, however, is that he did this with unyielding integrity. Taking over from disgraced former CEO Dennis Kozlowski, Breen began cleaning house. He did not, however, clean house the easy, political way. He didn't just talk about ethics; he took actions that demonstrated his commitment to operating with strong, unwavering values that would not be compromised for anyone or anything. His decision to replace the entire board of directors, for instance, was one example of his unyielding integrity. It would have been politically expedient to replace only some of the directors and enlist the others on his team to help with the transition. Breen, though, wanted all of them to resign. They resisted, of course, fearing that this mass resignation would make them appear guilty of wrongdoing and increase their legal liability.

Breen adroitly worked out an arrangement that allowed him to replace all the board members. Just as significantly, he filled the vacancies with an independent-minded, diverse group of directors. Breen also fired 290 of Tyco's 300 top managers during the first few months of his tenure, not because he felt they were guilty of unethical behavior but because their management approach was inconsistent with his vision for Tyco. They were part of a deal-making culture, and he was more interested in fostering a culture based on fiscal prudence and strong management principles and practices.

Clearly, eliminating so many top executives must have been a nightmare from a human resources standpoint and in terms of losing organizational knowledge. Breen, though, knew that whatever pain his integrity caused short term, it would benefit the company in the long run.

## An Employee Challenges the CEO

Gil joined a fast-growing, high-profile company as head of human resources. He had come from a more conservative, traditional organization where he had held a similar position. Though Gil enjoyed the eight years he spent at his previous employer, he felt the need for a fresh challenge and the opportunity to grow with a company that was growing.

It didn't take more than a few months on his new job for Gil to become uneasy with some of the new organization's policies and practices. Though he admired the CEO and his team for their savvy and aggressive strategies, he became uncomfortable with some of the shortcuts they asked him to support. For instance, the CEO wanted to bring in a senior financial person from another organization, with the ultimate aim of replacing the existing CFO. The CEO asked Gil to persuade the current CFO to take the new financial person under his wing and train him; the CEO stressed that Gil was not to give the CFO an inkling that he was training his successor. The CEO said that such information might be interpreted the wrong way, and they needed the current CFO to stay in his job for at least another two years.

Gil did not believe that this action (or the other questionable policies he was being asked to implement) was truly unethical, but it did violate his sense of the right way to do things—the way he had been taught to act. Gil didn't like shortcuts for the sake of expediency or a leadership style that favored manipulation over transparency. At the same time, the job was as challenging and rewarding as Gil had anticipated, and he didn't want to quit. It bothered him, though, that he was quietly going along with company policies he didn't really believe in.

Finally, he decided on a course of action. Not only did he express his concerns to the CEO, but he wrote a white paper analyzing how these policies ultimately had a negative impact on the company's bottom line. The CEO, of course, didn't agree with Gil, but he said he was open to talking about this subject more and that if Gil found himself balking at a request that rubbed him the wrong way, he should discuss his resistance with the CEO, and they would deal with it on a case-by-case basis. Though Gil was not going to change the company's policies, he had taken a stand that he was sure would be noted by the CEO and others in the organization and would result in his having greater freedom to function in ways that he felt comfortable with.

## How to Develop Unyielding Integrity

Some leaders have no interest in any kind of integrity, let alone the unyielding kind; they are nakedly ambitious, Machiavellian to the core. Others don't give integrity a thought, believing that they know right from wrong; they call it as they see it. It is impossible to develop integrity in both of these types, but fortunately they are rare. Most leaders who may appear to lack integrity often just lack awareness that they're acting without it. Once they become aware—once they become attuned to how and when they are behaving in ways that are inconsistent with their beliefs—they will be more likely to act with unyielding integrity. Here are some techniques that help foster this awareness:

• *Facilitate thinking about and discussing integrity issues.* The CEO and other senior leaders must make this subject part of an ongoing corporate dialogue. It is too late once the crisis hits to begin the process of discussing values and integrity. Examining integrity issues is like buying corporate insurance: deposits must be made in advance for when a future situation requires it. Addressing these issues means everything from developing intranet sites that examine the dilemmas leaders face when it comes to acting on their own beliefs to coaching that enables people to come to terms with their internal conflicts. It means leaders sharing their personal dilemmas and points of view about how they handle paradoxical, ethical, or questionable dilemmas. It also means acquiring the recognition that there is no single "right" point of view and that people need to take others' perspectives into consideration when examining their own sense of right and wrong.

At one company we know well, they work hard at catalyzing thought and discussion on the subject of ethics. Recently, this company agreed to purchase another company that produces a medical device regulated by the U.S. Food and Drug Administration. During the previous year some of the acquired company's products achieved scrutiny from regulatory agencies for potential design flaws that had affected a small number of patients. Though the flaw seemed minor to some people, relative to the potential good the product could contribute, the acquisition now presented a dilemma for everyone. Did the acquiring company fail to set a high enough standard? Did the acquirer create potential risk for itself in taking on this company and its issues?

As people debated these issues, the CEO of the acquiring company knew how Wall Street, the FDA, and investors would come down on the issues. But he asked a different—a higher-order—question: What would a patient, faced with a potential cure for his life-threatening disease, as well as knowledge of a potential risk, however small, say? What would any leader say if the patient were his own son or daughter? He wanted them to imagine the types of thoughts going through a patient's head and the risk-reward assessment that a patient would make, so his leaders could develop a point of view from a human perspective that was based on empathy with the patient. He wanted them to consider what the right thing to do is in this type of situation, that is, when the problem seems minor, relative to the greater good, and unlikely to cause people any serious problems, but when the problem seems no longer minor when viewed from the patient's perspective. Integrating this perspective into the corporate dialogue, then, provides another way of determining what the right thing to do is in these cases. In this particular case, the decision was to move forward with the acquisition, based on the belief that doing so was for the longer-term benefit of the patient.

• *Encourage people to articulate what they're thinking of doing before they do it.* When people write a blistering e-mail that states, "I quit! I can't work for a company that treats people the way this one does!" this dramatic resignation may seem noble and principled, but it may also be rash and melodramatic. Companies can lose highly principled leaders who act before they think—and before they talk about their plans. When leaders confine their thinking about integrity to their own heads, they have one-sided conversations. They can easily work themselves into an emotional reaction over an issue and act in a way that is ill-considered. By articulating their fears and reservations about an issue, though, they can receive reactions from others and perhaps adapt their point of view. Sometimes after hearing how others react, they may realize that they are not acting with unyielding integrity but with stubbornness and anger.

Leaders in the senior-level management of organizations know the hot-button issues—the ones where people are asked to make decisions or implement plans and projects that they don't personally agree with. Compliance, budgeting, cost-cutting, diversity-related decisions, bonus decisions, and promotions often bring issues of integrity to the surface. From top executives on down, leaders must ask others how they feel about these decisions and actions. Rather than maintain a polite silence, they should ask point-blank, "Does this bother you in any way?" This will enable and encourage people to think before they act.

• *Create a series of questions that help people grapple with what is right and help them find the courage to take the right course of action.* It takes serious reflection to determine what you believe and to find the courage to act on this belief. The following questions are designed to catalyze reflection:

Why are you taking a stand on this particular issue? Has an ideal you hold dear been violated? Does it seem as if you can't live with yourself if you don't take this stand?

Have you examined your motivation for making a decision or taking this action? Is this really a matter of integrity, or is there an element of self-interest involved?

Are you asked to do things by your boss or follow policies in line with organizational values that you find personally repugnant? Have you attempted to articulate your feelings about this subject to senior leaders? Have you looked for alternatives that might make your job more acceptable from a personal values perspective?

Do you feel your belief in the right and wrong way to do things at work has evolved over time? Have certain experiences allowed you to adapt and adjust your attitude, or are you so dug in that nothing will move you to consider another definition of what's right?

Do you distinguish between organizational-legal ethics and personal integrity? Are there situations in which you act in ways that conform to ethical behavior, as the board might interpret it, but still feel that you're doing something that goes against your principles?

What are the risks if you take a stand on this issue? How do you want people to interpret this action? What is it you are trying to "say"?

Our point is that thought-provoking questions and dialogue are often the best way to sort through complicated and difficult issues when a leader's integrity is at stake.

◆ ◆ ◆

We have now seen some of the challenges of leading with head, heart, and guts. These challenges demand a set of skills that are not easy to develop. In many instances, they demand even more than skill, they require that we act with integrity and become the very essence of who we are as leaders—and as human beings. They touch what we believe about ourselves, what we believe about others, and what we think is possible and desirable for the world and our future.

In the final part of our book, we will propose the idea of a "mature leader"—a whole leader, not a partial leader—who has not only experienced a lot of life but also has reflected a lot on life. A leader who understands the importance of acting intelligently with the wisdom of heart but who is not blinded by the heart, who has the courage to risk the ambiguity and complexity of leadership in today's world but is not foolhardy enough to believe that the right answers are risk-free and easy. In short, the mature leader is one who is willing to summon all the intelligence, empathy, and courage necessary to meet the demands of leading in the twenty-first century.

# Part Five

# MATURE LEADERSHIP

# 14

# DEVELOPING MATURE LEADERS FOR THE TWENTY-FIRST CENTURY

Throughout this book, we have been referring to holistic leaders and the need to develop the whole person. Although *holistic* is an appropriate term, *maturity* may be an even better one from a developmental standpoint. Mature leaders often display head, heart, and guts naturally. Based on years of experience, during which they had to deal with adversity and wrestle with a range of complex issues, these leaders have learned from these experiences and, consequently, have developed the wisdom that comes with maturity. As mature leaders, they don't simplistically over-rely on one aspect of their personality when faced with crucial decisions, as inexperienced or still-developing leaders often do. They don't rely exclusively on analysis when making strategic choices; they don't automatically shy away from taking risks in stressful situations, and they don't always ignore people issues in favor of results. In short, they are capable of more flexible, situational, and effective leadership actions. They have learned the hard way that being single-minded and rigid makes for bad leadership choices.

Maturity doesn't mean becoming one-third head, one-third heart, and one-third guts. Everyone has a natural leadership style, and a natural tendency to lean on intellect, emotion, or courage doesn't change with maturity. What *does* change is a willingness to consider options that don't fit with one's natural style. What also changes is a capacity for trying new ways of leading others and thus expanding the personal leadership capabilities. Often this isn't even a conscious choice. Maturity teaches us lessons that we integrate unconsciously into our leadership repertoire. After suffering enough setbacks when we bang our cognitive heads against a wall, we realize that there may be other ways that could be more successful— that it may be time to reflect, use compassion, try to connect with others emotionally and empathetically, and have the courage to be more transparent about who we are. We learn, over time, to stand up for what we feel is right rather than give in to what is politically expedient, because the more we learn about true leadership, the more we realize there is no other real choice.

Unfortunately, companies can't wait until all their leaders become mature. Ironically, by the time some companies have assembled a mature group of leaders, they frequently begin pushing for the next generation of leaders who are younger, more vital, and energetic. Waiting until a headstrong young leader becomes a wise sixty-year-old makes no sense for many reasons, not the least of which is that the young executive will probably leave the company long before he reaches maturity. Furthermore, leaders mature at different ages, so a thirty-five-year-old may be more mature than a sixty-year-old (and some people never gain leadership maturity).

Therefore, helping leaders at all ages develop this maturity is a necessity and is required in most companies to maintain a competitive edge. Having a cadre of skilled leaders who are aligned, understand the strategy, and live the values of the organization is one differentiator that must be built rather than bought.

The question confronting almost every company today is this: How do you develop leadership maturity? In each of the preceding chapters, we've suggested options for acquiring each capability. Here we want to focus specifically on some ways leaders can mature "prematurely"—in other words, ways in which the process of development can be accelerated by the leaders themselves, as well as through formal programs sponsored by the organization. Let's start out with a simple but often overlooked piece of advice: *Know whether your company has a head, heart, or guts culture*.

## What Companies Need

No leader should focus on developing equal measures of head, heart, and guts as if these qualities were ingredients listed in a cake recipe. Nor should companies believe that they need development programs that spend an equal amount of time on head, heart, and guts issues. No formula works for all companies and all leaders. Although a general goal of development should be to foster awareness and capability of all three qualities in leaders, a more specific goal is to tailor the approach to the culture and the individual.

Culturally, the majority of companies are head-oriented. They rely on data and focus on results, as might be expected in our performance-obsessed world. A significant minority, though, are heart-oriented, especially the not-for-profits and a growing number of companies that are led by executives with strong people values. Start-ups, high-techs filled with younger leaders, and companies with entrepreneurial cultures are often guts-oriented, that is, staffed by individuals who feel free to speak their mind and follow courses of action that are both risky and rooted in strong beliefs. While companies don't always fall neatly into one of these three categories, they usually have a dominant culture that is obvious to everyone who works there.

Development, therefore, should focus on helping the leadership population increase their capacity in the less dominant areas. Unfortunately, however, this rarely happens. Typically, leadership development is designed to reflect the dominant cultural orientation, providing learning consistent with the biases of the leadership population rather than stretching and challenging other dimensions.

But consider how former NYC mayor Rudy Giuliani and the New York City Police Department dramatically reduced crime in their city. For years, NYPD leaders possessed a guts orientation, not unlike most urban police department leaders. The quasi-militaristic style of leadership focused on closing ranks, taking strong positions, and showing courage; there was a macho culture within the ranks. Giuliani, though, improved the police department's performance by helping leaders acquire a more analytic (cognitive) approach to their work. They implemented disciplined management practices, conducted sophisticated examinations of crime data, targeted certain communities based on specific crime patterns, and deployed police and other department services based on their analyses. Leaders were encouraged to use a variety of tools to fight crime, but their choices were always informed by the data. Most observers attribute the dramatic reduction of crime in New York, at least in part, to these practices. By using their heads as well as their guts, the NYPD command created a model that has now been applied in other police departments in this country and around the world.

Insurance underwriting is another example where the leadership has shifted from an orientation of guts and instinct to a more analytical approach to the work. Good underwriters were once those who had a sixth sense about an applicant, and those who succeeded made more right choices than wrong. Today, you cannot succeed as an underwriter without sophisticated analytical skills. Leaders in the insurance industry must encourage the use of data, statistical analyses, and fact-based decision making.

The Bank of America has always been very execution-focused and performance-driven. In fact, the company is a remarkable example of how to re-engineer complex processes to dramatically increase customer service, quality, and delivery. However, banking, like the retail, airline, and hospitality industries, relies on a "factory model" for delivery: large numbers of front-line workers interact with the customer daily, but their developmental needs and career aspirations are too often ignored. Today, one of the challenges facing Bank of America is how to develop and grow front-line associates. Most companies know that their brand and the company's values are transmitted through employees who touch customers on the front line. Getting this right requires both data (head) to analyze the potential impact that this connection can have on customer satisfaction and engagement (heart), especially with workers who, because of lower pay and shorter tenure, can easily move down the street to join another company. To their credit as an industry leader, Bank of America is engaging in widespread leadership development with this population to blend head, heart, and guts capability in their leadership, to grow market share, retain key people, and remain an innovator in financial services.

Avon Products would be described by most as a traditional heart culture in which relationships have played a central role in how the business operates. The company's unrelenting focus on their representatives' experience has been one of the key factors in their success. However, the leadership at Avon has realized that this quality of the culture is insufficient to continue their growth. They are moving to a model that we would describe as more focused on the head and guts. Without losing their hearts, leaders are now being compelled to demonstrate more analytical discipline and courage in making tough decisions than ever before. Leaders at Avon today must be capable of making hard decisions based on the facts and taking more risks, while retaining those values of the culture that have made it great.

Most companies are both the beneficiary and the victim of their strong cultures, which can oftentimes prevent leaders from going against the conventional wisdom, standard practice, or tradition. Levi Strauss is a good example of an overly compassionate, family-owned enterprise that found it difficult to displace American jobs, as textile manufacturing moved rapidly to countries where labor costs were lower. When Levi's finally realized that it was impossible to maintain a competitive price due to their high, fixed overhead costs, it was already too late. Their revenues had declined from $7 billion to almost $4 billion, and their products were no longer the industry standard. Fortunately, today the company is rebuilding its unique fashion cachet and market position. But their downward spiral probably created a significantly larger loss of jobs and market share because they were demonstrating too much compassion and heart.

A counterexample is Enron, which created a culture without compassion and emphasized the intellect. Their single-minded focus on hiring and developing the smartest guys in the room resulted in the company outsmarting itself. Every industry is faced with the dilemma of managing compassion and making tough decisions, but keeping both dimensions in balance is what makes leadership an art and a challenge.

From an individual perspective, certain leaders are predisposed to act primarily with their head, heart, or gut, and they need to know their preference and work at expanding their repertoire. A head-oriented leader may be in charge of a project team of similarly like-minded people, but management knows that it will take guts to make this project successful. Analytical ability alone will not get the team where it needs to go. This head-oriented leader must develop guts or he is bound to fail.

Most people can easily identify their own tendencies to lead with head, heart, or guts. Although many may fool themselves about how adept they are at using the two less-dominant modes, they generally can tell you where they lean when making key leadership decisions. Therefore, one goal in developing leadership maturity is to help leaders recognize how over-reliance on their dominant mode prevents them from being successful. This goal can be achieved through coaching, as well as more formal leadership development programs. And sometimes particularly introspective people can do it on their own by reflecting on their failures and understanding how their singular approach caused them to make critical mistakes.

What motivates leaders to want to develop themselves outside their preferred mode, though, is understanding the risks if they don't. Here are three common reasons for singular leadership failure:

• *A disconnect between what you know you should do and what you actually do*. Many times, when we have asked a leader why she made a decision that was clearly the wrong one and what she was thinking about in connection with this decision, her response was something like the following: "I knew it was the wrong approach, but it's how I've always done it and couldn't see other alternatives." This limited range of responses can undermine any leader's ability to succeed, especially when you consider the wide variety of situations and challenges most leaders face as part of their jobs. Contrary to expectations, many leaders realize that they should depart from their usual way of doing business, but they are in a rut. To extricate themselves, they need to be aware of approaches to problem solving that involve other leadership modes and make a willful effort to employ them when necessary.

• *Misdiagnosis*. Failure may result from a poor understanding of whether head, heart, or guts leadership is called for in a given situation. Cross-culturally, North American leaders make the wrong diagnosis frequently. For instance, more than one company has attempted to break into the heart-based Latin American market using a cognitive approach. U.S. business leaders arrive there armed with spread sheets and product specs, and they want to plunge into data-based conversations with Latin colleagues as a way to improve performance. What many South American executives want, though, is to know the people they're going to be working with. They want to understand who the other people are, learn about their families, and establish a more personal relationship before they get down to business. There are similar cross-cultural differences nearly everywhere in the world. Too many leaders are blind to these differences and don't take them seriously until they begin to interfere with their ability to get a job done. The inability to apply all three qualities—head, heart, and guts—can be particularly problematic in working across cultural boundaries.

• *Creation of false expectations*. Some leaders are capable of operating out of all three leadership modes, but they lack the transparency necessary to communicate this fact to other people. They appear to be cool, tough, and results-oriented, but underneath their professional exterior beats the heart of a values-driven, mission-oriented leader. When they display compassion, however, transcending their managerial role and letting others in, people are confused; they didn't expect their boss to act this way; they may even see the behavior as odd; they fail to respond as expected, so the behavior doesn't have the desired effect. Confused direct reports are reluctant to trust this type of leader, because they may feel he is being manipulative, or at least inconsistent. Mature leaders, on the other hand, are more transparent in communicating who they are and how they lead. They apply all three modes appropriately as the situation calls for and reduce the risk of confusing others.

Given all this, companies must make it a priority to go beyond the development norm and help leaders build their capacity to exhibit head, heart, and guts as complete leaders—at the right times in the right situations. Here are a range of ways they can do so.

## How Organizations Can Help Leaders Mature

Laura Tyson and Nigel Andrews wrote an article to which we referred earlier. They noted how poorly equipped today's MBAs are to become global leaders. Though they acknowledged that many of these MBAs were very smart, they concluded that more than intellect was required to be successful as a global leader. Equally important were the personal characteristics that these future leaders possessed. Because MBA programs emphasize cognitive learning, students emerge with a strong knowledge base, but from the standpoint of the other qualities we've discussed regarding heart and guts, they are ill prepared to meet the challenges of leading in a global environment. They will not have the skill they need to manage cultural differences, work with people from diverse backgrounds, and deal with situations that are fraught with ambiguity and uncertainty.

MBAs are, of course, only one pool of candidates from which companies draw their future leaders, albeit an important one. Unfortunately, the pool can be rather shallow when it comes to recruiting people with the potential to become mature leaders. Whether a company is hiring MBAs, new college graduates, or experienced professionals, we would argue that they need to establish hiring criteria that go beyond intelligence and technical skills. Though we strongly believe that head, heart, and guts qualities can be developed, we also believe it is much easier to develop them in certain people than others. This leads us to our first suggestion:

• *Hire based on criteria related to head, heart, and guts.* This may seem like a daunting task. How do you determine whether a recent business school graduate has the type of guts companies require? It is actually easier than it might seem. If, for instance, you want to know whether someone has heart capacity, an interviewer should ask candidates questions based on the four elements of emotional intelligence:

1. Self-Awareness

    How would those who know you best describe your strengths and weaknesses?

    How have you applied what you know about yourself to achieve success, either in school or at work?

    Why do you think it's important to be self-aware? What difference does it make? How has it made a difference to you?

2. Self-Regulation

    How do you respond when you are under pressure?

    Who are you at your worst? What are those emotions that can undermine your success if you don't manage them effectively?

    What types of situations create the most stress for you? In what circumstances are you most vulnerable?

3. Empathy

    How effectively are you able to put yourself in other people's shoes and understand what they're going through?

What approach do you take to identify with other people's perspectives?

How are you able to identify with people's problems, even when they are very much different from your own?

How do you express understanding and compassion in a way that helps others?

4. Managing Conflict and Influencing

How well do you deal with people who don't agree with you?

How do you manage to disagree with others without having a situation flare into open warfare?

What types of conflicts are the most difficult for you to manage?

What are the ways in which you garner influence with others, particularly those over whom you have no direct authority?

Obviously, these questions can be tailored to different people and situations. And as anyone who has ever conducted selection interviews knows, it would be important to pull for examples of the qualities that people say they have. The point, though, is that it is possible, as well as desirable, to select people based on their heart.

Similarly, guts can be assessed by asking questions such as these:

If you had to decide whether to downsize the workforce or face a precarious financial situation, would you be willing to let people go if you had worked with them for years and were personally close? How would you approach this situation?

If an opportunity suddenly arose to buy a great company to which you had outsourced a lot of business, how would you ensure that you moved quickly enough, even though you lacked the time to gather all the information you might want to move forward?

> Can you describe a situation in your personal life when you made a decision that entailed a certain amount of risk? What was at stake? How did you handle the situation? How did you analyze the trade-offs? How did it turn out?

In terms of intellect and knowledge (head), companies need to go beyond the traditional candidate assessments. Yes, it's important to know where a candidate ranked in his class and the types of intellectual capabilities that were reflected in his classroom performance. The assessment, though, should also address some of the less traditional traits that we have enumerated. For instance, is he likely to think in unorthodox ways about traditional organizational boundaries? Has he demonstrated an ability to do so in school and in other aspects of his life? How has he exhibited practical judgment? Has he demonstrated an ability to do rather than just think? What has he accomplished outside school? Has he engaged in activities that have made real contributions—that indicate an ability to take an idea from conception to reality?

• *Encourage people not to be prisoners of their own experience.* Experience is important for developing leadership maturity, but it becomes counterproductive when the experience is narrow or when people don't make the effort to learn from it. Head, heart, and guts evolve from a wide range of experiences and an openness to learning from them. Companies are now making it clear, therefore, that leaders are expected to think and act globally, to travel, to be open to global assignments, to be part of teams that include cross-functional work, and to venture into areas and take on assignments where the risk of failure is significant. Too often, companies communicate explicitly or implicitly that avoiding failure and building success upon success in one function are the keys to getting ahead. Here are three ways to encourage people to break out from a narrow experience range:

• *Involve them in action learning experiences that force them to take on new and challenging assignments.* We run Action Learning programs every week for companies throughout the world. We have learned that creative program designs that involve putting people in a temporary system of new values and ways of doing things can stimulate insights about oneself, the business, and the world. Action learning can create conditions in which head, heart, and guts are integrated through conflict, feedback, assessment, real work, and other methods. These programs may force a heart-oriented leader to confront learning situations where the only way to succeed is to balance risk and reward or to make a strong stand based on values within a learning community. We have found that action learning can stretch people on multiple levels, often requiring participants to use capacities that are rarely called for in their "day jobs."

• *Place people in jobs before they're ready to handle them*. Clearly, this action needs to be taken carefully. If the majority of people in an organization are in stretch assignments, big problems will result. Selectively, however, companies can develop certain leaders who seem to have the capacity for integrating head, heart, and guts behaviors but haven't had the chance to do so because their previous jobs haven't challenged them sufficiently, or they are placed in new leadership roles only when they are "ready now." By placing them in roles that they aren't quite ready for, they will have to learn on the job and probably rely on more than what they've experienced. They will be forced to experiment with new behaviors to handle the jobs.

• *Provide them with coaching and other tools that facilitate learning from experience*. Two people can have the same background and very similar work experiences, yet one emerges as a mature leader and the other doesn't. Why? Normally this happens because one person is able to reflect and integrate the learning that comes from the experience. This means making a conscious effort to examine key experiences and figure out what was done right, what was done wrong, and how a similar experience might be handled better the next time. This type of learning often requires help. Deeply honest, politically incorrect discussions can enhance learning. Too often, conversations among team members, or even between bosses and direct reports, are sugar-coated and evasive. No one says to a prospective leader, "We almost missed the deadline because you are too cautious." People are worried about crossing the line and getting too personal. Real learning, though, requires people to confront their weaknesses. They need to understand their gaps—where they lack heart or where their analysis was useless because it wasn't followed by actions. Coaching fosters these types of eye-opening conversations and provides opportunities for reflection. Coaches are skilled in getting people to think and talk honestly about their experiences, and this can enable them to cull learning from a situation that would otherwise escape them.

• *Develop leaders with the head, heart, and guts traits in mind.* The qualities we have described in the previous chapters aren't the only ones that help develop mature leaders, but they provide a good foundation. We've chosen these in particular because they represent a cross-section of head, heart, and guts and because we have witnessed how useful they are in helping leaders think and act in more holistic ways.

Finally, we should reiterate a point we made in Chapter Two: *Develop people with a larger framework in mind.* A heart-focused culture needs to develop its leaders differently from the way a head-based culture does. Similarly, an established, Fortune 500 company that is struggling with mediocre financial results has different development needs from those of a younger, entrepreneurial company that wants to retain its best and brightest people as it grows. And of course, an arrogant, command-and-control executive may need to focus on heart issues, while an overly cautious leader may want to key in on guts.

To keep all these elements in mind, we often use a framework that helps companies analyze the needs of the organization going forward, how these needs affect leadership requirements, and what these requirements are (roles, skills, knowledge, and behaviors). This framework also addresses the leadership development architecture, including individual development issues and collective learning processes and incorporates structural matters into the mix, looking at everything from succession planning to performance management.

Whether you use this type of framework or some other approach, recognize that you can't develop head, heart, and guts leaders without understanding all of the touch points in your organization. If you don't develop people systematically—if your approach ignores all the systems and processes that influence development—you are unlikely to achieve the goal of infusing your organization with leadership maturity.

## The Next Step in Leadership Development

Given the continuing search for talent and the increasing importance of multifaceted, situational leaders, organizations must focus on leadership development as never before. It is no longer enough to employ an off-the-shelf development program or to assume that it will suffice if you send someone to a business school program or rotate high-potential leaders through various assignments. In fact, companies delude themselves into thinking that these ad hoc methods result in anything more than small, incremental gains in leadership value.

We're not just blaming organizations for this tactical approach. Those of us in the leadership development business have been too quick to apply solutions and tools without considering the bigger picture. As useful as 360-degree feedback and other methods can be, they don't represent breakthroughs. In fact, during the last twenty-five years, we have not seen any quantum leaps forward in development methodology.

We believe that the head, heart, and guts framework represents a breakthrough of sorts in describing in reasonably straightforward terms what just about every smart CEO is saying: "Get me more leaders who are smart, who have good people skills, and who have the courage of their convictions." They don't want just one of these qualities; they need all three. These CEOs can't afford to wait until leaders mature and develop over a period of many years. They need to accelerate the process, and nothing out there is helping them do it.

Most organizations are filled with partial leaders like the supersmart executive who never says what he believes or the empathetic senior vice president who is unable to get things done. What we all want are whole leaders, and companies are gradually coming to the realization that this type of leadership cannot be created by classroom training alone. Gradually, companies are identifying and seeding the organization with people capable of displaying head, heart, and guts. Over time all of us will contribute to developing the tools, insights, and instruments needed to recruit, train, and develop whole leaders who are able to deliver whole solutions to the world's challenges, unencumbered by partial leadership styles and philosophies. When this happens, all of us will be happier and the world will be a more productive and prosperous place to live.

# References

Badaracco, J., Jr. (1997). *Defining moments: When managers must choose between right and right.* Boston: Harvard Business School Press.

Bartz, C. (2005, May). *Fortune.*

Bossidy, L., & Charan, R. (2002). *Execution: The discipline of getting things done.* New York: Crown Press.

Bossidy, L., & Charan, R. (2004). *Confronting reality: Doing what matters to get things right.* New York: Crown Press.

Cashman, K. (1998). *Leadership from the inside out.* Provo, UT: Executive Excellence Publishing.

Charan, R., Drotter, S., & Noel, J. (2001). *The leadership pipeline: How to build the leadership-powered company.* San Francisco: Jossey-Bass.

Dotlich, D. L., & Cairo, P. C. (2003). *Why CEOs fail: The 11 behaviors that can derail your climb to the top—and how to manage them.* San Francisco: Jossey-Bass.

Dotlich, D. L., Noel, J. L., & Walker, N. (2004). *Leadership passages: The personal and professional transitions that make or break a leader.* San Francisco: Jossey-Bass.

Flaum, S. (2004). *Pharmaceutical Executive.*

Florida, R., & Goodnight J. (2005, July–Aug.). Managing for creativity. *Harvard Business Review.*

Friedman, T. L. (2005). *The world is flat: A brief history of the twenty-first century.* New York: Farrar, Straus and Giroux.

Groppel, J. L. (1999). *The corporate athlete: How to achieve maximal performance in business and life.* New York: Wiley.

Harman, S. (2004, Jan.). *Harvard Business Review.*

Hogan, R., Curphy, C. J., & Hogan, J. (1994). *American Psychologist, 49,* 493–504.

Johnson, B. (1992). *Polarity management: Identifying and managing unsolvable problems.* Amherst, MA: Human Resource Development Press.

Kim, W. C., & Mauborgne, R. (1993, Spring). Making global strategies work. *Sloan Management Review.*

Kirkpatrick, S., & Locke, E. (1991). *Academy of Management Journal, 5,* 48–59.

Klein, M., & Napier, R. (2003). *The courage to act: Five factors of courage to transform business.* Mountain View, CA: Davies-Black Publishing.

Kuhn, T. S. (1996). *The structure of scientific revolutions.* Chicago: University of Chicago Press.

Lencioni, P. (2002). *The five dysfunctions of a team.* San Francisco: Jossey-Bass.

Loehr, J., & Schwartz, T. (2003). *The power of full engagement.* New York: Free Press.

Ludeman, K., & Erlandson, E. (2004, May). Coaching the alpha male. *Harvard Business Review.*

McGregor, D. (1960). *The human side of enterprise.* New York: McGraw-Hill.

Mercer Delta Executive Learning Center. Access: http://elc.mercerdelta.com

Roddick, A. (2003). *A revolution in kindness.* West Sussex, England: Anita Roddick Books.

Rosenthal, R. (1994). Interpersonal expectancy effects: A 30-year perspective. *Current Directions in Psychological Science, 3*(6), 176–179.

Schank, R. (1997). *Virtual learning: A revolutionary approach to building a highly skilled workforce.* New York: McGraw-Hill.

Schectman, M. R. (1994). *Working without a net: How to survive and thrive in today's high-risk business world.* Englewood Cliffs, NJ: Prentice Hall.

Taylor, F. (1911). *The principles of scientific management.* New York: Harper.

Wheatley, M. (2001). *Leadership and the new science.* San Francisco: Berrett-Koehler.

# About the Authors

*David L. Dotlich* is president of the Mercer Delta Executive Learning Center, a leading global provider of senior executive programs throughout the world. He also consults to executive committees, CEOs, and senior leaders of such companies as Johnson & Johnson, Nike, Bank of America, Intel, Toshiba, Ernst & Young, and Novartis. He is coauthor of five best-selling leadership books: *Why CEOs Fail: The 11 Behaviors That Can Derail Your Climb to the Top—and How to Manage Them; Action Coaching: How to Leverage Individual Performance for Company Success; Unnatural Leadership: Going Against Intuition and Instinct to Develop Ten New Leadership Instincts; Action Learning: How the World's Top Companies Are Re-Creating Their Leaders and Themselves;* and *Leadership Passages: The Personal and Professional Transitions That Make or Break a Leader* (all published by Jossey-Bass).

*Peter C. Cairo* is a consultant who specializes in the areas of leadership development, executive coaching, and organization effectiveness. He has served as a consultant and coach to senior executives and leadership teams at Merck, Avon Products, Colgate-Palmolive, and others. Cairo spent twenty years on the faculty of Columbia University, where he served as chairman of the Department of Organizational and Counseling Psychology. He is coauthor of *Why CEOs Fail: The 11 Behaviors That Can Derail Your Climb to the Top—and How to Manage Them; Unnatural Leadership: Going Against Intuition and Instinct to Develop Ten New Leadership Instincts;*

and *Action Coaching: How to Leverage Individual Performance for Company Success.*

*Stephen H. Rhinesmith* is a partner in the Mercer Delta Executive Learning Center, a firm that specializes in assessing, coaching, and developing global leaders. He is an expert on global business–strategy implementation and human resource development. Rhinesmith is a consultant to many Fortune 100 corporations on globalization and the development of global mindsets, competencies, and corporate cultures. He is author of *A Manager's Guide to Globalization.*

# Index